Microso
Access 2
Brief Ed

INTERAC
SERIES

Kenneth C. Laud
Jason Eiseman

Azimuth Interactive, inc.

**Irwin
McGraw-Hill**

Boston   Burr Ridge, IL   Dubuque, IA   Madison, WI   New York   San Francisco   St. Louis
Bangkok   Bogotá   Caracas   Lisbon   London   Madrid   Mexico City   Milan   New Delhi   Seoul
Singapore   Sydney   Taipei   Toronto

McGraw-Hill Higher Education

A Division of The **McGraw-Hill** Companies

MICROSOFT ACCESS 2000 BRIEF EDITION
Copyright © 2000 by The McGraw-Hill Companies, Inc. All rights reserved. Printed in the United States of America. Except as permitted under the United States Copyright Act of 1976, no part of this publication may be reproduced or distributed in any form or by any means, or stored in a data base or retrieval system, without the prior written permission of the publisher.

 This book is printed on recycled, acid-free paper containing 10% postconsumer waste.

RECYCLED

2 3 4 5 6 7 8 9 0 QPD/QPD 9 0 9 8 7 6 5 4 3 2 1 0 9

ISBN   0-07-234075-4

Vice president/Editor-in-Chief: *Michael W. Junior*
Sponsoring editor: *Trisha O'Shea*
Developmental editor: *Kyle Thomes*
Senior marketing manager: *Jodi McPherson*
Project manager: *Carrie Sestak*
Production supervisor: *Michael R. McCormick*
Senior freelance design coordinator: *Laurie Entringer*
Supplement coordinator: *Matthew Perry*
Compositor: *Azimuth Interactive, Inc.*
Typeface: *10/12 Sabon*
Printer: *Quebecor Printing Book Group/Dubuque*

Library of Congress Catalog Card Number: 99-62020

http://www.mhhe.com

Microsoft® Access 2000
Brief Edition

INTERACTIVE COMPUTING SERIES

Kenneth C. Laudon
Jason Eiseman

Azimuth Interactive, Inc.

At **McGraw-Hill Higher Education**, we publish instructional materials targeted at the higher education market. In an effort to expand the tools of higher learning, we publish texts, lab manuals, study guides, testing materials, software, and multimedia products.

At **Irwin/McGraw-Hill** (a division of McGraw-Hill Higher Education), we realize technology will continue to create new mediums for professors and students to manage resources and communicate information with one another. We strive to provide the most flexible and complete teaching and learning tools available and offer solutions to the changing world of teaching and learning.

Irwin/McGraw-Hill is dedicated to providing the tools necessary for today's instructors and students to navigate the world of Information Technology successfully.

Seminar Series - Irwin/McGraw-Hill's Technology Connection seminar series offered across the country every year, demonstrates the latest technology products and encourages collaboration among teaching professionals.

Osborne/McGraw-Hill - A division of the McGraw-Hill Companies known for its best-selling Internet titles *Harley Hahn's Internet & Web Yellow Pages* and the *Internet Complete Reference*, offers an additional resource for certification and has strategic publishing relationships with corporations such as Corel Corporation and America Online. For more information, visit Osborne at www.osborne.com.

Digital Solutions - Irwin/McGraw-Hill is committed to publishing Digital Solutions. Taking your course online doesn't have to be a solitary venture. Nor does it have to be a difficult one. We offer several solutions, which will let you enjoy all the benefits of having course material online. For more information, visit www.mhhe.com/solutions/index.mhtml.

Packaging Options - For more about our discount options, contact your local Irwin/McGraw-Hill Sales representative at 1-800-338-3987, or visit our Web site at www.mhhe.com/it.

Preface

Goals/Philosophy

The *Interactive Computing Series* provides you with an illustrated interactive environment for learning software skills using Microsoft Office. The Interactive Computing Series is composed of both text and multimedia interactive CD-ROMs. The text and the CD-ROMs are closely coordinated. *It's up to you. You can choose how you want to learn.*

Approach

The *Interactive Computing Series* is the visual interactive way to develop and apply software skills. This skills-based approach coupled with its highly visual, two-page spread design allows the student to focus on a single skill without having to turn the page. A running case study is provided through the text, reinforcing the skills and giving a real-world focus to the learning process.

About the Book

The **Interactive Computing Series** offers *two levels* of instruction. Each level builds upon the previous level.

Brief lab manual - covers the basics of the application, contains two to four chapters.

Introductory lab manual - includes the material in the Brief textbook plus two to four additional chapters. The Introductory lab manuals prepare students for the *Microsoft Office User Specialist Proficiency Exam (MOUS Certification)*.

Each lesson is organized around **Skills**, **Concepts**, and **Steps (Do It!)**.

Each lesson is divided into a number of Skills. Each **Skill** is first explained at the top of the page.
Each **Concept** is a concise description of why the skill is useful and where it is commonly used.
Each **Step (Do It!)** contains the instructions on how to complete the skill.

About the CD-ROM

The CD-ROM provides a unique interactive environment for students where they learn to use software faster and remember it better. The CD-ROM is organized in a similar approach as the text: The **Skill** is defined, the **Concept** is explained in rich multimedia, and the student performs **Steps (Do It!)** within sections called Interactivities. There are at least 45 Interactivities per CD-ROM. Some of the features of the CD-ROM are:

Simulated Environment - The Interactive Computing CD-ROM places students in a simulated controlled environment where they can practice and perform the skills of the application software.
Interactive Exercises - The student is asked to demonstrate command of a specific software skill. The student's actions are followed by a digital "TeacherWizard" that provides feedback.
SmartQuizzes - Provide performance-based assessment of the student at the end of each lesson.

Using the Book

In the book, each skill is described in a two-page graphical spread (Figure 1). The left side of the two-page spread describes the skill, the concept, and the steps needed to perform the skill. The right side of the spread uses screen shots to show you how the screen should look at key stages.

Figure 1

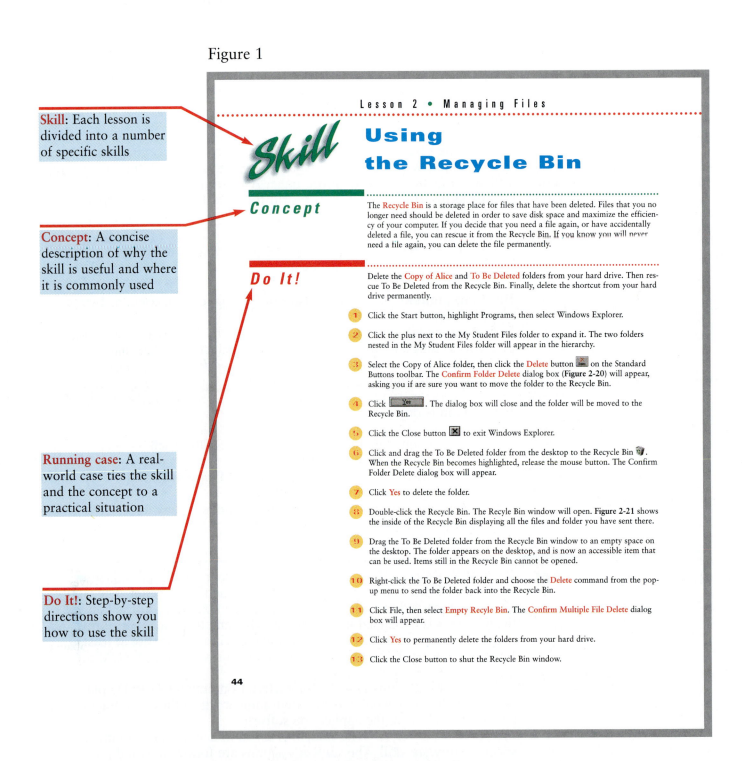

Skill: Each lesson is divided into a number of specific skills

Concept: A concise description of why the skill is useful and where it is commonly used

Running case: A real-world case ties the skill and the concept to a practical situation

Do It!: Step-by-step directions show you how to use the skill

Lesson 2 • Managing Files

Skill Using the Recycle Bin

Concept

The Recycle Bin is a storage place for files that have been deleted. Files that you no longer need should be deleted in order to save disk space and maximize the efficiency of your computer. If you decide that you need a file again, or have accidentally deleted a file, you can rescue it from the Recycle Bin. If you know you will never need a file again, you can delete the file permanently.

Do It!

Delete the Copy of Alice and To Be Deleted folders from your hard drive. Then rescue To Be Deleted from the Recycle Bin. Finally, delete the shortcut from your hard drive permanently.

1. Click the Start button, highlight Programs, then select Windows Explorer.

2. Click the plus next to the My Student Files folder to expand it. The two folders nested in the My Student Files folder will appear in the hierarchy.

3. Select the Copy of Alice folder, then click the Delete button on the Standard Buttons toolbar. The Confirm Folder Delete dialog box (Figure 2-20) will appear, asking you if you are sure you want to move the folder to the Recycle Bin.

4. Click Yes . The dialog box will close and the folder will be moved to the Recycle Bin.

5. Click the Close button to exit Windows Explorer.

6. Click and drag the To Be Deleted folder from the desktop to the Recycle Bin. When the Recycle Bin becomes highlighted, release the mouse button. The Confirm Folder Delete dialog box will appear.

7. Click Yes to delete the folder.

8. Double-click the Recycle Bin. The Recyle Bin window will open. Figure 2-21 shows the inside of the Recycle Bin displaying all the files and folder you have sent there.

9. Drag the To Be Deleted folder from the Recycle Bin window to an empty space on the desktop. The folder appears on the desktop, and is now an accessible item that can be used. Items still in the Recycle Bin cannot be opened.

10. Right-click the To Be Deleted folder and choose the Delete command from the pop-up menu to send the folder back into the Recycle Bin.

11. Click File, then select Empty Recycle Bin. The Confirm Multiple File Delete dialog box will appear.

12. Click Yes to permanently delete the folders from your hard drive.

13. Click the Close button to shut the Recycle Bin window.

44

End-of-Lesson Features

In the book, the learning in each lesson is reinforced at the end by a quiz and a skills review called Interactivity, which provides step-by-step exercises and real-world problems for the students to solve independently.

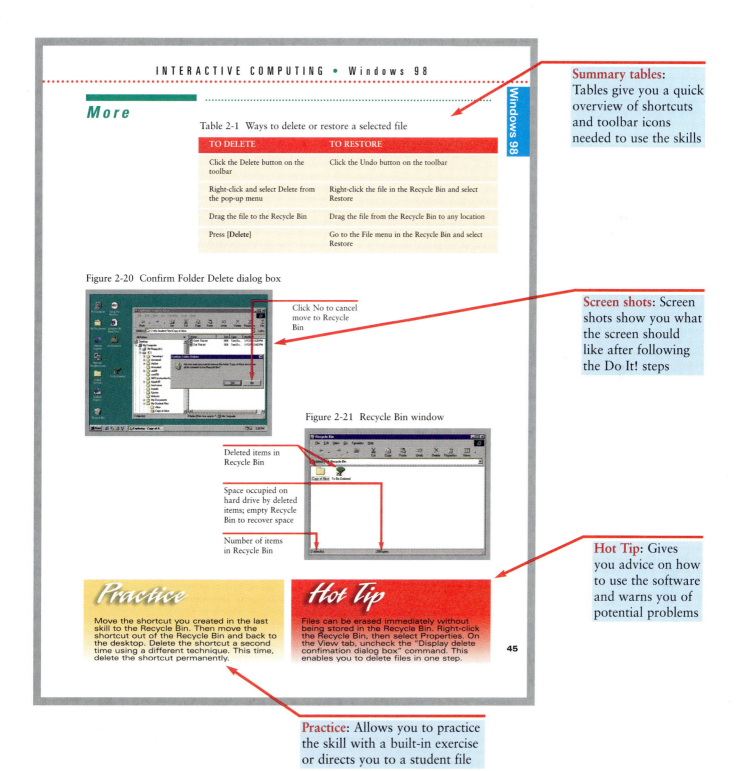

Windows 98

More

Table 2-1 Ways to delete or restore a selected file

TO DELETE	TO RESTORE
Click the Delete button on the toolbar	Click the Undo button on the toolbar
Right-click and select Delete from the pop-up menu	Right-click the file in the Recycle Bin and select Restore
Drag the file to the Recycle Bin	Drag the file from the Recycle Bin to any location
Press [Delete]	Go to the File menu in the Recycle Bin and select Restore

Figure 2-20 Confirm Folder Delete dialog box

Click No to cancel move to Recycle Bin

Figure 2-21 Recycle Bin window

Deleted items in Recycle Bin

Space occupied on hard drive by deleted items; empty Recycle Bin to recover space

Number of items in Recycle Bin

Practice

Move the shortcut you created in the last skill to the Recycle Bin. Then move the shortcut out of the Recycle Bin and back to the desktop. Delete the shortcut a second time using a different technique. This time, delete the shortcut permanently.

Hot Tip

Files can be erased immediately without being stored in the Recycle Bin. Right-click the Recycle Bin, then select Properties. On the View tab, uncheck the "Display delete confimation dialog box" command. This enables you to delete files in one step.

45

Summary tables: Tables give you a quick overview of shortcuts and toolbar icons needed to use the skills

Screen shots: Screen shots show you what the screen should like after following the Do It! steps

Hot Tip: Gives you advice on how to use the software and warns you of potential problems

Practice: Allows you to practice the skill with a built-in exercise or directs you to a student file

Using the Interactive CD-ROM

The Interactive Computing multimedia CD-ROM provides an unparalleled learning environment in which you can learn software skills faster and better than in books alone. The CD-ROM creates a unique interactive environment in which you can learn to use software faster and remember it better. The CD-ROM uses the same lessons, skills, concepts, and Do It! steps as found in the book, but presents the material using voice, video, animation, and precise simulation of the software you are learning. A typical CD-ROM contents screen shows the major elements of a lesson (see Figure 2 below).

Skills list: A list of skills allows you to jump directly to any skill you want to learn or review, including interactive sessions with the TeacherWizard

Figure 2

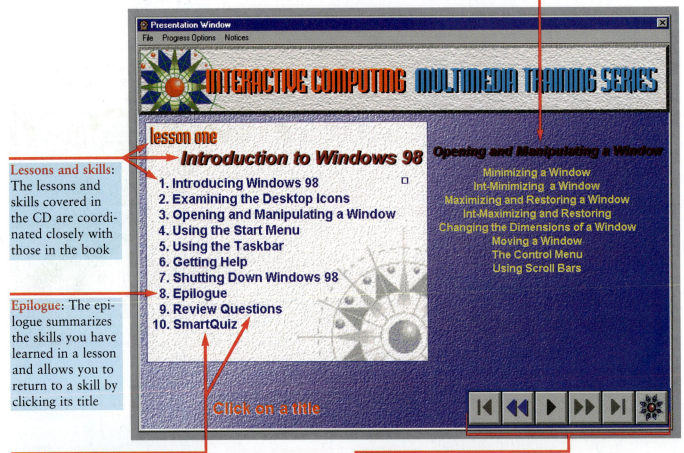

Lessons and skills: The lessons and skills covered in the CD are coordinated closely with those in the book

Epilogue: The epilogue summarizes the skills you have learned in a lesson and allows you to return to a skill by clicking its title

Review Questions and **SmartQuiz**: Review Questions test your knowledge of the concepts covered in the lesson; SmartQuiz tests your ability to accomplish tasks in a simulated software environment

User controls: Precise and simple user controls permit you to start, stop, pause, jump forward or backward one sentence, or jump forward or backward an entire skill. A single navigation star takes you back to the lesson's table of contents

Unique Features of the CD-ROM: TeacherWizard™ and SmartQuiz™

Interactive Computing: Software Skills offers many leading-edge features on the CD currently found in no other learning product on the market. One such feature is *interactive exercises* in which you are asked to demonstrate your command of a software skill in a precisely simulated software environment. Your actions are followed closely by a digital TeacherWizard that guides you with additional information if you make a mistake. When you complete the action called for by the TeacherWizard correctly, you are congratulated and prompted to continue the lesson. If you make a mistake, the TeacherWizard gently lets you know: "No, that's not the right icon. Click on the Folder icon on the left side of the top toolbar to open a file." No matter how many mistakes you make, the TeacherWizard is there to help you.

Another leading-edge feature is the end-of-lesson SmartQuiz. Unlike the multiple choice and matching questions found in the book quiz, the SmartQuiz puts you in a simulated digital software world and asks you to show your mastery of skills while actually working with the software (Figure 3).

Figure 3

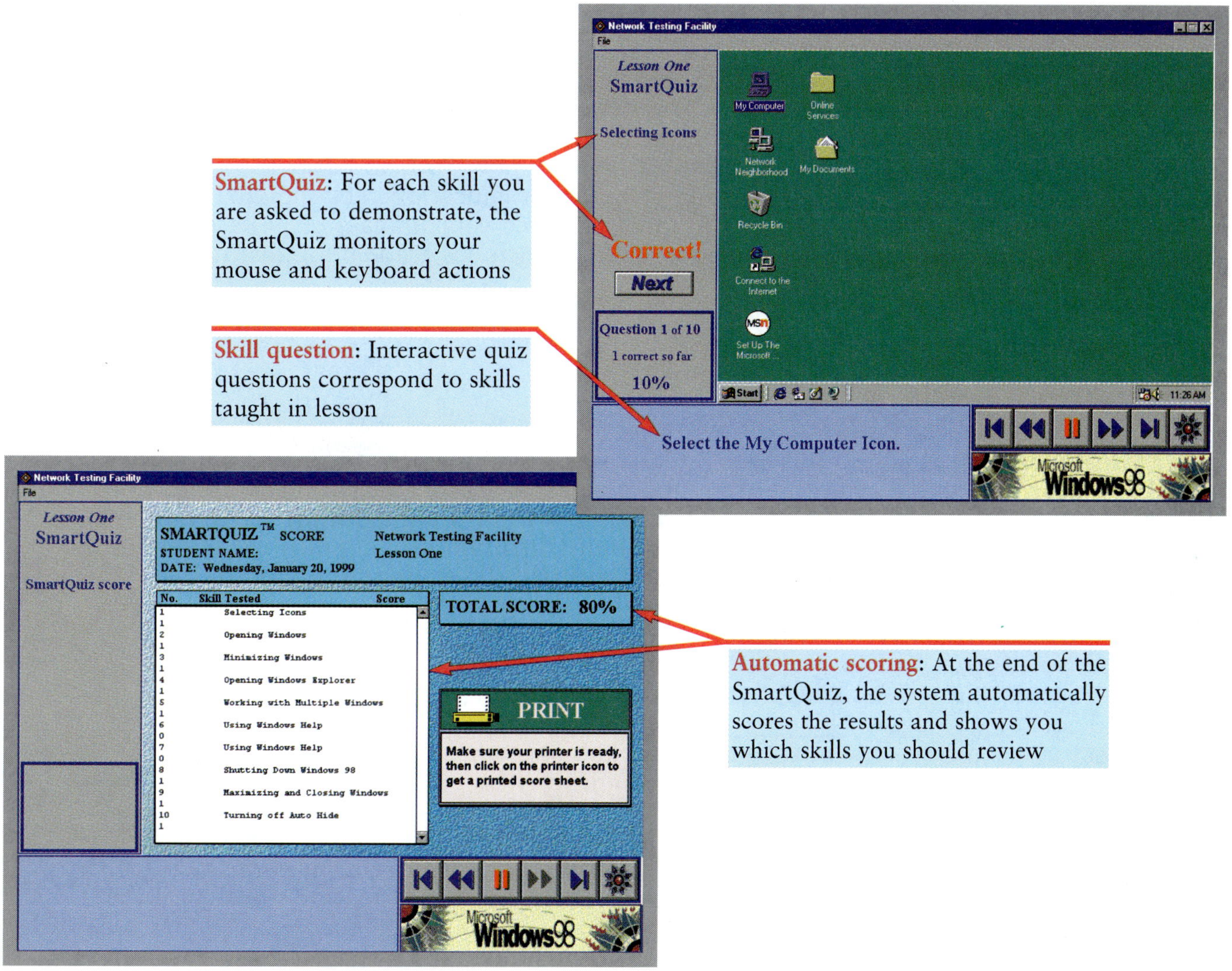

SmartQuiz: For each skill you are asked to demonstrate, the SmartQuiz monitors your mouse and keyboard actions

Skill question: Interactive quiz questions correspond to skills taught in lesson

Automatic scoring: At the end of the SmartQuiz, the system automatically scores the results and shows you which skills you should review

ix

Teaching Resources

The following is a list of supplemental material available with the Interactive Computing Series:

ATLAS Active Testing and Learning Assessment Software - available for the Interactive Computing Series, is our cutting edge "Real TimeAssessment" software. ATLAS is web-enabled and allows students to perform timed tasks while working live in an application. ATLAS will track how a specific task is completed and the time it takes to complete that task. ATLAS measures Proficiency and Efficiency ("It's not only what you do but how you do it."). ATLAS will provide full customization and authoring capabilities for professors, and includes content from all of our application Series.

Instructor's Resource Kits

The Instructor's Resource Kit provides professors with all of the ancillary material needed to teach a course. Irwin/McGraw-Hill is dedicated to providing instructors with the most effective instruction resources available. Many of these resources are available at our Information Technology Supersite www.mhhe.com/it. Our Instructor's Kits are available on CD-ROM and contain the following:

Network Testing Facility (NTF) - Tests acquired software skills in a safe simulated software environment. NTF tracks a student score and allows the instructor to build screens that indicate student progress.

Diploma by Brownstone - is the most flexible, powerful, and easy-to-use computerized testing system available in higher education. The diploma system allows professors to create an Exam as a printed version, as a LAN-based Online version, and as an Internet version. Diploma includes grade book features, which automate the entire testing process.

Instructor's Manual - Includes:
-Solutions to all lessons and end-of-unit material
-Teaching Tips
-Teaching Strategies
-Additional exercises.

Student Data Files - To use the Interactive Computing Series, students must have Student Data Files to complete practice and test sessions. The instructor and students using this text in classes are granted the right to post the student files on any network or stand-alone computer, or to distribute the files on individual diskettes. The student files may be downloaded from our IT Supersite at www.mhhe.com/it.

Series Web Site - Available at www.mhhe.com/cit/apps/laudon.

Digital Solutions

Pageout Lite - is designed if you're just beginning to explore Web site options. Pageout Lite is great for posting your own material online. You may choose one of three templates, type in your material, and Pageout Lite instantly converts it to HTML.

Pageout - is our Course Web site Development Center. Pageout offers a Syllabus page, Web site address, Online Learning Center Content, online exercises and quizzes, gradebook, discussion board, an area for students to build their own Web pages, and all the features of Pageout Lite. For more information please visit the Pageout Web site at www.mhla.net/pageout.

OLC/Series Web Sites - Online Learning Centers (OLCs)/Series Sites are accessible through our Supersite at www.mhhe.com/it. Our Online Learning Centers/Series Sites provide pedagogical features and supplements for our titles online. Students can point and click their way to key terms, learning objectives, chapter overviews, PowerPoint slides, exercises, and web links.

The McGraw-Hill Learning Architecture (MHLA) - is a complete course delivery system. MHLA gives professors ownership in the way digital content is presented to the class through online quizzing, student collaboration, course administration, and content management. For a walk-through of MHLA visit the MHLA Web site at www.mhla.net.

Packaging Options - For more about our discount options, contact your local Irwin/McGraw-Hill Sales representative at 1-800-338-3987 or visit our Web site at www.mhhe.com/it.

Visit www.mhhe.com/it
THE ONLY SITE WITH ALL YOUR CIT AND MIS NEEDS.

Acknowledgments

The Interactive Computing Series is a cooperative effort of many individuals, each contributing to an overall team effort. The Interactive Computing team is composed of instructional designers, writers, multimedia designers, graphic artists, and programmers. Our goal is to provide you and your instructor with the most powerful and enjoyable learning environment using both traditional text and new interactive multimedia techniques. Interactive Computing is tested rigorously in both CD and text formats prior to publication.

Our special thanks to Trisha O'Shea and Kyle Lewis, our Editors for computer applications and concepts. Both Trisha and Kyle have poured their enthusiasm into the project and inspired us all to work closely together. Kyle Thomes, our Developmental Editor, has provided superb feedback from the market and excellent advice on content. Jodi McPherson, marketing, has added her inimitable enthusiasm and market knowledge. Finally, Mike Junior, Vice-President and Editor-in-Chief, provided the unstinting support required for a project of this magnitude.

The Azimuth team members who contributed to the textbooks and CD-ROM multimedia program are:

Ken Rosenblatt (Textbooks Project Manager and Writer, Interactive Writer)
Raymond Wang (Interactive Project Manager)
Russell Polo (Programmer)
Michele Faranda (Textbook design and layout)
Jason Eiseman (Technical Writer)
Larry Klein (Contributing Writer)
Thomas Grande (Editorial Assistant, layout)
Stefon Westry (Multimedia Designer)

Contents

Access 2000 Brief Edition

Contents

Continued

L E S S O N

1

INTRODUCTION TO DATABASES

Microsoft Access is a computer application that makes it possible for you to construct powerful systems for organizing information, called databases. An Access database allows you to record data, maintain it, edit it, and add to it using simple commands and procedures. The objects you create using the program will facilitate your ability to work with stored information in a number of highly useful ways. Most importantly, because Access provides the opportunity to relate databases to one another, you can share information among objects in a database, or even among separate databases.

Using Access, you will learn how to create a functioning database made up of several components, called database objects, each of which serves a specific purpose. In doing so, you will explore the application and become familiar with its basic elements and operations. Later on, Access' more advanced features, such as table relationships, will augment your ability to work with a database. If you require assistance while using Access, the application includes an extensive help facility, as well as the possibility to access online support via the World Wide Web.

CASE STUDY
Kyle Dawson is a database consultant who has been hired by Stay Fast, Inc. to design a database that will store information about the company's employees. Stay Fast is a reseller of nuts, bolts, and other fasteners, buying them in bulk from manufacturers and reselling them to retail stores, construction companies, and contractors. A paper system served the company well when it had only 15 employees, but it has grown to fifty employees and wants to convert to an electronic database system before expanding any further. Database consultants like Kyle are often hired to set up a database and to teach employees how to use it. Trained employees of the business can then maintain and expand the database.

Introducing Database Software

Concept

Microsoft Access is a program that allows you to build computerized databases, which are systems for storing, organizing and retrieving information. Though you may not realize it, you are probably already familiar with many noncomputerized databases, such as paper records kept in filing cabinets, or your own personal address book. Computer databases can store the same information as traditional paper databases, but they organize it in a more flexible form, storing it in a computerized grid or table.

For example, your address book might have lines for a friend's first and last name, address, phone number, and birthday. In a computerized database, the same information is stored differently. Each column, or field, in a database table contains a specific type of information. So, each line from an address book entry, such as your friends' last names, would form a separate column in the table. In turn, all of the lines of information about this friend would make up a single row across the table, called a record (see **Figure 1-1**). A computerized address book would then have the details for each category — name, address, and so on — common to all entries entered down a column, and the complete body of information for any single person entered across a row.

There are many advantages to using computerized databases. One advantage is in the added ease and flexibility of entering and working with data. Just as you can edit text in a word processor or numbers on a spreadsheet, you can easily change data that you enter into a database, adding, deleting, or moving information on screen.

Stored information is, of course, useful only if it can be easily retrieved. One of the greatest advantages of computerized databases is that they offer several ways to retrieve information. For instance, unlike traditional address books, a computerized address database would not limit the user to searching by a person's last name (see **Figure 1-2**). Instead, you could perform searches based on other fields, such as phone number, and even perform searches based on two or more fields at once. For example, you could find all of the people in the database who live in the same state but have different area codes. Furthermore, if the information you seek is spread across separate databases, you can link tables with common data and perform a comprehensive search.

Figure 1-1 Table in an Access database sorted by Last Name

Last Name	Phone #	First Name	Address1	City	State	Zip
Albeiro	(813) 585-4731	Frank	65 Thunder Alle	Clearwater	FL	34615
Carson	(619) 256-6732	Andrea	56 Longwater S	San Diego	CA	92114
Dershkovitz	(203) 329-6548	Allison	12 Firehouse R	Stamford	CT	6905
Gheri	(208) 376-9467	Larry	1667 Highland A	Boise	ID	83702
Gustavson	(218) 724-5832	Mark	4 White Castle .	Duluth	MN	55803
Hendsleydale	(212) 727-8612	Martin	677A E. 12 St.	New York	NY	12204
Korngold	(404) 372-0091	Hume	131 Jarlsberg R	Atlanta	GA	30322
Lambert	(212) 7278612	Carla	222 Charles St.	New York	NY	12204
Land	(901) 332-3322	Grace	3734 Elvis Pres	Memphis	TN	38116
Mitzelflik	(901) 314-8712	Francois	12 Wayside Ter	Chamburg	TN	38105
Planck	(334) 724-9246	Maxmillian	14 Proust St.	Tuskegee	AL	36083
Smith	(602) 968-7765	Samuel	44 Porter Pl.	Tempe	AZ	85281

Record: 1 of 12

A single record

A field

Figure 1-2 Table in an Access database sorted by State

State	Last Name	First Name	Address1	City	Zip	Phone #
AL	Planck	Maxmillian	14 Proust St.	Tuskegee	36083	(334) 724-9246
AZ	Smith	Samuel	44 Porter Pl.	Tempe	85281	(602) 968-7765
CA	Carson	Andrea	56 Longwater S	San Diego	92114	(619) 256-6732
CT	Dershkovitz	Allison	12 Firehouse R	Stamford	6905	(203) 329-6548
FL	Albeiro	Frank	65 Thunder Alle	Clearwater	34615	(813) 585-4731
GA	Korngold	Hume	131 Jarlsberg R	Atlanta	30322	(404) 372-0091
ID	Gheri	Larry	1667 Highland A	Boise	83702	(208) 376-9467
MN	Gustavson	Mark	4 White Castle .	Duluth	55803	(218) 724-5832
NY	Lambert	Carla	222 Charles St.	New York	12204	(212) 7278612
NY	Hendsleydale	Martin	677A E. 12 St.	New York	12204	(212) 727-8612
TN	Mitzelflik	Francois	12 Wayside Ter	Chamburg	38105	(901) 314-8712
TN	Land	Grace	3734 Elvis Pres	Memphis	38116	(901) 332-3322

Record: 1 of 12

Access 2000

Starting Access

Concept

Before you can view or modify a database, you must open the Access application. Unlike other Windows programs, Access does not open with a blank file ready to be used. Instead, it offers you the choice of creating a new database or opening an existing one.

Do It!

In order to open the sample database that he wishes to view, Kyle must first start Access.

1 Click **Start** on the Windows taskbar. The Start menu appears.

2 Move the mouse pointer over the Start menu to **Programs**, then click **Microsoft Access** on the submenu that appears, as shown in **Figure 1-3**. Access will open. **Figure 1-4** shows the opening screen that will appear. Since Windows allows for customization, your menus may appear differently than the ones shown, and your startup procedure may vary slightly from the one demonstrated here.

3 Click **OK** to affirm the default option, **Open an Existing Database**. The Open dialog box (**Figure 1-5**) appears, allowing you to determine which file is to be opened.

4 Click the **Look in** drop-down list arrow, then select the drive containing your **Student Files** folder from the drop-down list of drives and folders that appears. (Ask your instructor if you cannot locate these files.)

5 Open the **Student Files** folder. Its contents will be displayed in the main area of the dialog box.

6 Click **Doit1-2** to select it, then click **Open** Access will open the database and display the Database window, shown in **Figure 1-6**.

Figure 1-3 Opening Access from the Start menu

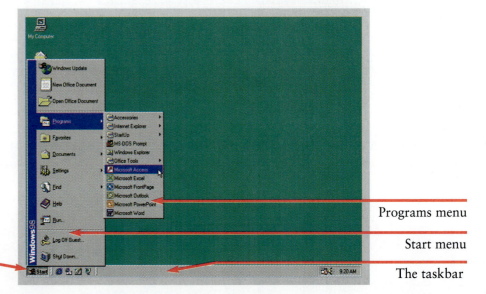

Programs menu

Start menu

Start button

The taskbar

Figure 1-4 Access dialog box

If a database has been opened before, its file name may appear here; simply select it and click OK to open it

Figure 1-5 Open dialog box

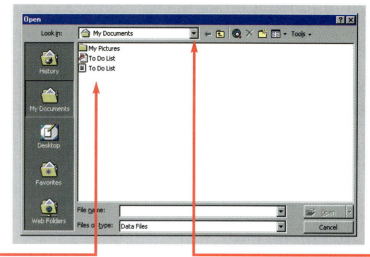

The files and/or folders that are located in the selected drive or folder will appear here

Click here to select the drive on which your Student Files reside

Figure 1-6 Database window

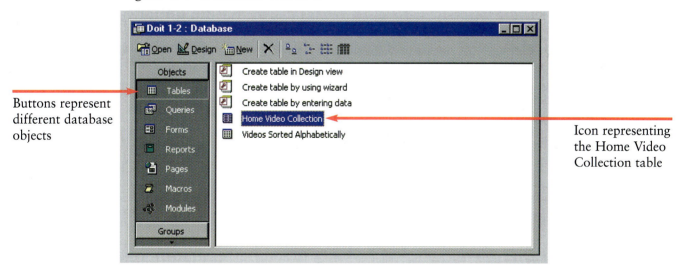

Buttons represent different database objects

Icon representing the Home Video Collection table

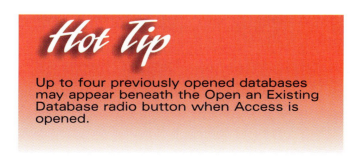

Hot Tip

Up to four previously opened databases may appear beneath the Open an Existing Database radio button when Access is opened.

Opening an Existing Database

Concept

There are several ways Access allows you to find databases which you were previously working on. Some files may be saved in the Access folder, and some may be saved in other folders on your computer.

Do It!

1 Kyle wants to find a database which was saved in a folder outside of the Access folder.

2 Click the Open existing database button 📂. The Open dialog box appears.

3 Click the Look In drop down arrow list. Click the C: option, seen in **Figure 1-7** This option allows you to look in folders in your C: drive, which contains files which have been saved to your computers' hard drive.

4 Double-click the Program Files folder.

5 Double-click the Microsoft Office folder.

6 Double-click the Office folder.

7 Double-click the samples folder.

8 Double-click on the fpnwind database to open it. This reveals a list of sample tables to choose from, seen in **Figure 1-8**. Double-click on the Categories table to open it.

More

Once you have created and saved your own databases using Access, every time you open it you will have the option of opening a database you were working on before.

Access will list the databases you have worked on, starting with the most recent, when you first open Access. Click the database you choose to work on, and click open, Access will open directly to the database you have chosen.

Figure 1-7 Look in: window in the Open dialog box

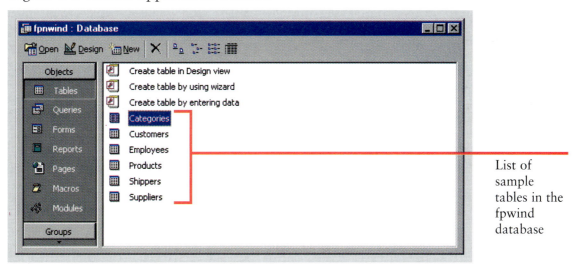

Drive or folder
which is
currently being
searched

Drive or folder
which will be
selected

Access 2000

Figure 1-8 Access application window

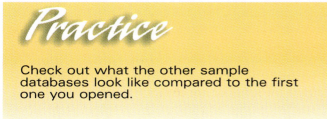

List of
sample
tables in the
fpwind
database

Practice

Check out what the other sample
databases look like compared to the first
one you opened.

Hot Tip

If you click on History in the Open dialog
box, it will list all of the programs you have
worked on in Access, including the dates
and times you worked on them.

AC 1.7

Exploring the Access Window

Concept

When a database is opened, the Database window will appear in the Access window, as shown in **Figure 1-9**. The Database window is the main control center for building and controlling a database.

The Database window contains the following buttons, each of which relates to a specific database object:

- Tables: give a database its basic structure, storing data and fields in a tabular form

- Queries: allow you to specify instructions for selecting specific data from one or more tables

- Forms: electronic data entry sheets that usually contain the fields that comprise a single record; usually make data entry and editing easier by resembling the paper data entry forms that they are designed to replace

- Reports: used to present processed data in an organized manner

- Pages: specifies the total number of pages in a form or report

- Macros: allow you to define and execute a series of actions that automate certain frequently used database tasks

- Modules: incorporated programs that allow powerful and specialized automation of Access operations

The rest of the Access application window contains the following screen elements:

- Title bar: contains the application Control menu icon, the name of the application, and the sizing buttons (Minimize, Maximize/Restore, and Close)

- Sizing buttons: located on the title bar and control how you view their window. The Maximize button displays the window at the size of the entire screen, while the Minimize button reduces the window to its program button on the Windows 98 taskbar. The Restore button replaces the Maximize button, and makes the window revert to its previous size when clicked.

- Menu bar: contains the names of menus which, when clicked, present lists of commands from which to choose

- Database toolbar: contains graphical buttons which execute specific commands when clicked

- Status bar: appears at the bottom of the screen and displays the activity being undertaken, as well as indicating whether or not certain features are currently active

Figure 1-9 The Access application window

Title bar

Menu bar

Database
toolbar

Sizing buttons

Click here to
open and view
a selected item

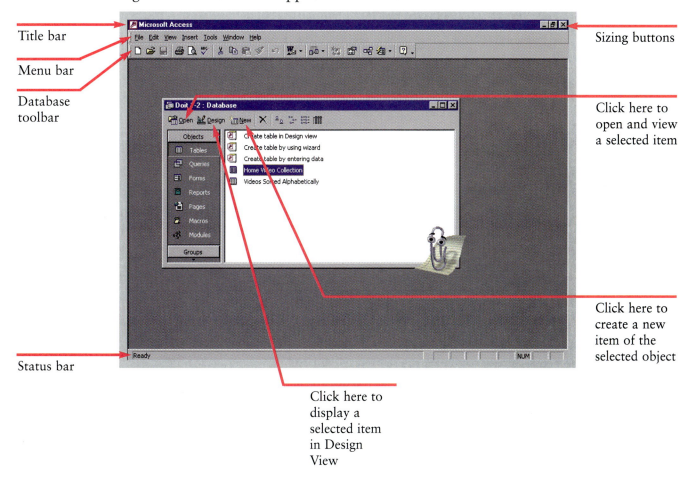

Click here to
create a new
item of the
selected object

Status bar

Click here to
display a
selected item
in Design
View

Hot Tip

When the mouse pointer is paused over a
button on a toolbar, Access will display a
small box called a ScreenTip that contains
the name of the indicated button.

Previewing and Printing a Table

Concept

Once you have entered all of your information in a table, it might be useful to Print the database you have created. Before you print anything you should check the document in Print Preview. Print Preview will help you make any changes that must be made before you print, with respect to the format of your database.

Do It!

Kyle is satisfied with his document, and he's ready to print it. First, he is going to make sure the format fits his needs in Print Preview.

1. Open the sample database, Suppliers.

2. Click File. Click Print Preview (see **Figure 1-10**). This is what your table will look like when it is printed.

3. To change the layout of the page, click File, then click Page Setup. A dialog box will appear. Click the Page tab at the top of the dialog box. Click the Landscape orientation radio button, as seen in **Figure 1-11**. Then click OK.

4. Instead of taking up three pages of printed paper, the table now only takes up two, so you are ready to print. Click File, then click Print. The Print dialog box appears (see **Figure 1-12**).

5. Click OK to accept the default settings and you will print your table.

More

The Page Setup dialog box may also be used to change margins. If part of one page spills over onto a second page, simply changing right and left margins may be all that is needed to fit everything on one page.

If the Page Setup dialog box does not open to the Margins tab, click the Margins tab to bring it to the front of the dialog box.

You may also choose to print only certain pages in a document. By changing the default settings in the Print dialog box you can print one page of a multiple page document. You can also print some, but not all of a multiple page document.

Figure 1-10 Print Preview window

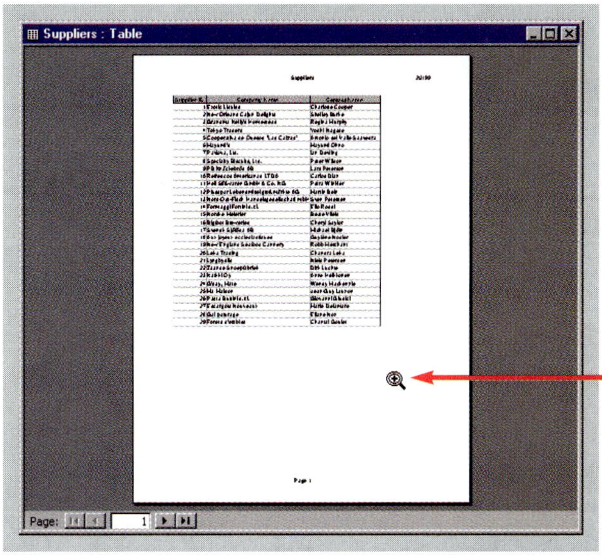

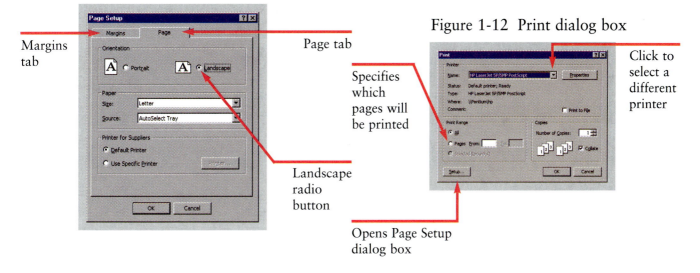

Magnifying tool allows you a closer look at your document

Figure 1-11 Page Setup dialog box

Margins tab

Page tab

Figure 1-12 Print dialog box

Click to select a different printer

Specifies which pages will be printed

Landscape radio button

Opens Page Setup dialog box

Practice

Print a copy of the sample database table, Employees.

Hot Tip

You may also use the Page Setup dialog box to print unusually sized papers. Click the size drop-down list, and select the size and style of paper on which you are printing.

Getting Help Using the Office Assistant

Concept

The Office Assistant is an animated interface that allows you to access Access' powerful Help features

Do It!

Kyle will use the Office Assistant to find out more about Access' help facilities.

1 Click Help, then click Show the Office Assistant. If the Office Assistant is already visible, click the Office Assistant.

2 Type tips with the office assistant into the text entry field, as shown in **Figure 1-13**.

3 Click ⊙ Search . A list of possible help topics appears above the question you entered.

4 Click the third radio button, Display tips, and messages through the Office Assistant. **Figure 1-14** shows the Microsoft Access window that will appear.

5 Read the Help topic pertaining to the Office Assistant, clicking a few of the help buttons next to additional topics to find out more.

6 When you have finished reading about some of the Office Assistant's capabilities, click the Close button in the upper-right corner of the dialog box.

7 Click Help again, then click Hide the Office Assistant, to hide the Assistant.

More

From time to time the Assistant will offer you tips on how to use Access more efficiently. The appearance of a small light bulb, either in the Assistant's window or on the Office Assistant button, indicates that there is a tip to be viewed. To see the tip, click the light bulb in whichever location it appears.

The Office Assistant can be customized. Click the ⊙ Options button in its dialog balloon to open the Office Assistant dialog box. This dialog box has two tabs: Gallery and Options. The Gallery tab contains eight assistants you can choose from, and scrolling through the characters provides you with a preview of each one. From the Options tab, shown in **Figure 1-15**, you can alter the Assistant's capabilities and decide what kinds of tips it will show.

Figure 1-13 Office Assistant

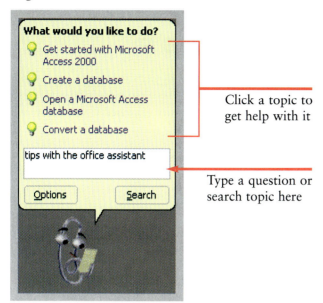

Click a topic to get help with it

Type a question or search topic here

Figure 1-14 Help with the Office Assistant

Click to get additional help with the specified topic

Figure 1-15 Office Assistant dialog box

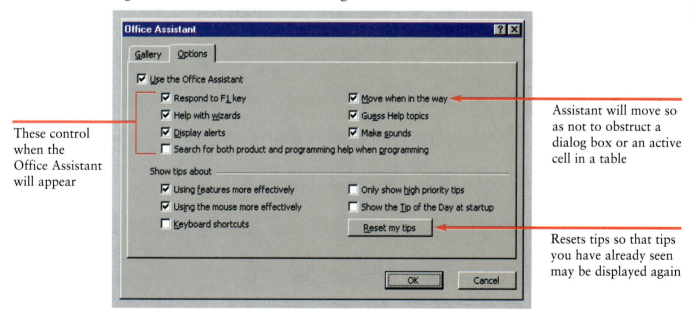

These control when the Office Assistant will appear

Assistant will move so as not to obstruct a dialog box or an active cell in a table

Resets tips so that tips you have already seen may be displayed again

Practice

Use the Office Assistant to learn about moving the Office Assistant and its balloon.

Hot Tip

The Office Assistant is common to all Office 2000 applications. Therefore, any Assistant options you change will affect it in all Office programs.

Getting Help in Access

Concept

Access has more traditional help facilities that are easily searched if you know what you are looking for. Once you have selected a topic supplied by the Office Assistant it is not difficult to find the other help features.

Do It!

Kyle wants to use the Index to find out more about ScreenTips.

1. Click the Office Assistant. Type **Ways to get assistance while you work?** Then click **Search**.

2. Position the pointer over the bullet labeled **Ways to get assistance while you work** and click. A window appears, as shown in **Figure 1-16**. Click the icon in the upper-left hand corner to open the **Index**.

3. Click the **Index** tab to bring it to the front, as shown in **Figure 1-17**.

4. The Index scrolls if you type in the text box, anticipating your selection.

5. Type **Ways to get assistance while you work**, the Index will present you with a list of topics. Double-click on any topic to learn more about it.

6. When you are finished reading, click the window's **Close** button.

More

The Index tab of the Help topics dialog box is very helpful if you know what the task you are trying to accomplish is called, or if you know the name of the feature that you want to find out more about. If you are unsure of exactly what you are looking for, the **Contents** tab of the Help Topics dialog box may be a better option for you. The Contents feature contains every Help topic that Access offers, broken down by category, and is useful if you wish to obtain a broad view of the topics available. The **Answer Wizard** tab allows you to search for key words found in Help topics to pinpoint those topics that might be most helpful.

Figure 1-16 Microsoft Access Help topics

Click to open the Index

Clicking an item such as this opens a large ScreenTip to more thoroughly explain the topic

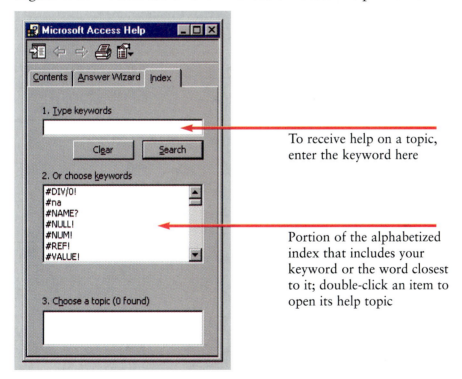

Figure 1-17 Index tab of the Microsoft Access Help feature

To receive help on a topic, enter the keyword here

Portion of the alphabetized index that includes your keyword or the word closest to it; double-click an item to open its help topic

Practice

Use the Index to find a shortcut key that relates to the Office Assistant.

Hot Tip

If your computer is connected to the Internet, you can access Microsoft's Web pages directly from Access. Click the Help menu, and then click Office on the Web. Finally, click a topic to go to its Web page.

Closing a File and Exiting Access

Concept

It is important to properly exit the Access program when you are finished with the day's session. Correctly closing the application will help you avoid any data loss.

Do It!

1 Kyle has finished using Access for the day and is ready to exit the application.

2 Click File, then click Exit (see **Figure 1-18**). Access closes and removes itself from the desktop. If the database that was open had been altered in any way, Access would have first prompted you to save changes before closing.

More

There are other ways you can close a file and exit Access. The easiest method is to use the Close buttons ☒ located in the upper-right corner of the window. The Close button on the menu bar is for the active workbook, and the Close button on the title bar is for the application. Also located on the title bar is the Control menu. This menu can be accessed by clicking the Access icon at the left end of the title bar, which is shaped like a key, and houses the Restore, Move, Size, Minimize, Maximize and Close commands.

You may open any menu on the menu bar by pressing [Alt] followed by the underlined letter in the menu's title. You will notice that menu commands also have a letter in their name underlined; typing the underlined letter will activate its command on the open menu. For example, with the File menu open, typing [o] will bring up the Open dialog box to open a database, while pressing [x] will exit Access.

Figure 1-18 Exiting the application

Close command on the File menu

Exit command on the File menu

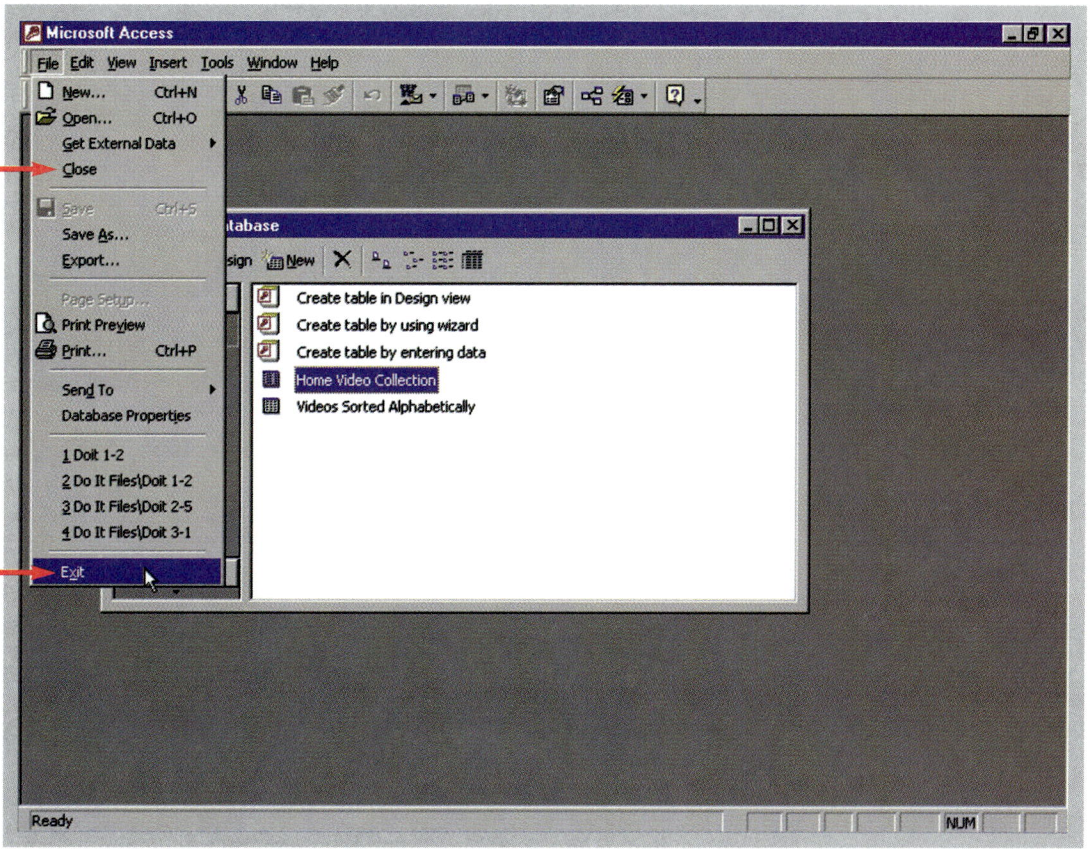

Practice

Open Access from the Start menu, close the Microsoft Access dialog box by clicking the close button, then close Access by using the Control menu.

Hot Tip

Right-clicking anywhere on the title bar will produce the Control menu, while double-clicking the title bar will maximize or restore the window's size.

Shortcuts

Function	Button/Mouse	Menu	Keyboard
Open a database	📂	Click File, then click Open Database	[Ctrl]+[O]
Minimize a window	_	Click Control icon, then click Minimize	
Maximize a window	□	Click Control icon, then click Maximize	
Restore a maximized window	⧉	Click Control icon, then click Restore	
Close a window	✕	Click Control icon, then click Close	[Alt]+[F4] (application window only)
Help	?	Click Help, then click Microsoft Access Help	[F1]
What's This?		Click Help, then click What's This?	[Shift]+[F1]

Identify Key Features

Name the items indicated by callouts in **Figure 1-19.**

Figure 1-19 Components of the Access window

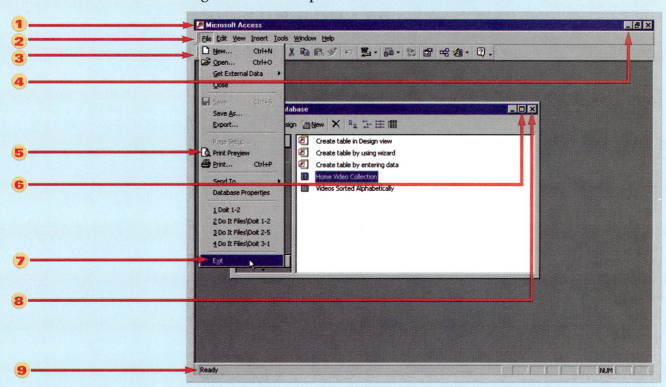

Select The Best Answer

10. Contains a window's Control menu icon

11. Database table element that holds one specific type of information

12. Main control center for working with an Access database

13. Gives a database its basic structure

14. Animated help feature that offers tips and answers questions

15. The Print Preview command is found in this menu

16. Use this to change the view of the table

17. You have to use it to change the page format

a. Page Setup

b. Office Assistant

c. File

d. Field

e. Database window

f. Scroll bar

g. Table

h. Title bar

Complete the Statement

18. A complete set of information contained in one row of a database table is called a:

    a. Field

    b. Form

    c. Record

    d. Column

19. All of the following are Access database objects except:

    a. Table

    b. Field

    c. Form

    d. Report

20. A database object that allows you to automate frequently executed tasks is a:

    a. Query

    b. Wizard

    c. Shortcut

    d. Macro

21. The Index feature lets you search for help topics:

    a. Alphabetically

    b. By asking questions

    c. By category

    d. By key word

22. Information regarding your current activity in Access appears in the:

    a. Database toolbar

    b. Menu bar

    c. Status bar

    d. Title bar

23. You can use all of the following to exit Access except:

    a. The Database window Close button

    b. The application window Close button

    c. The File menu

    d. The Control menu

24. Print Preview mode is best used to:

    a. Edit information in a table

    b. Change the format of your database

    c. See what your table will look like when printed

    d. See what your document will look like in other programs

25. The quickest way to find a specific record in your document is to:

    a. Use the scroll arrows to carefully check the table line by line.

    b. Type the number of the record you are looking for

    c. Click on the scroll bars and quickly scan the table

    d. To minimize the number of records in your table

26. When you first open Access you have the option of choosing:

    a. A sample database to work on

    b. The most recent databases saved in Access

    c. A comprehensive list of every database ever worked on in Access

    d. Nothing, Access automatically opens a blank database

Interactivity

Test Your Skills

1. Start the Microsoft Access application and browse an existing database:

   a. Use the Start menu to begin using Access.

   b. Open the database file you used earlier, **DoIt 1-2**.

   c. Click each of the object buttons in the Database window to view the titles of the existing objects (some buttons may be empty).

   d. Return to the Tables button when you are done.

2. Use Microsoft Access' Help features:

   a. Ask the **Office Assistant** for information on **designing a database**.

   b. View one of the topics provided by the Assistant.

   c. Use the **Contents** tab to read the help topics listed under the category **Creating a Database and Working in the Database Window**.

   d. Use the **Index** tab to find information on viewing **What's This?** tips.

   e. Use **What's This?** to obtain a ScreenTip about the Exit command on the File menu.

3. Print a database table:

   a. Open the database file you used earlier, **DoIt 1-2**.

   b. View the database in **Print Preview** mode.

   c. Practice making changes in the appearance of the document, by changing the margins in **Page Setup**.

   d. Print the table.

4. View different records in a long database table:

   a. Open the sample database, Products.

   b. Find record 53.

   c. Use the **scroll arrows** to find record 71.

   d. Use the **record selector buttons** to jump to the last record, then the first record.

   e. Use the **scroll arrows** to explore all of the fields in the table.

5. Exit Access:

   a. Use the application window's Close button to exit Access.

   b. If you have altered the database file in any way, do not save the changes.

Interactivity (continued)

Problem Solving

Congratulations! You have been hired by Ruloff and DeWitt, a rapidly growing advertising agency that specializes in promoting new products and services. For your first project as a Marketing and Research Assistant, you will compile data on the magazine preferences of a cross section of people. This data will eventually be stored and maintained in an Access database. Your initial assignment is to plan the database on paper following appropriate design principles. First, make a list of the fields that should be included in the database. To get you started, here is a list of suggested fields: a unique identification number for each record, first name, last name, age, gender, occupation, number of magazine titles read regularly, favorite magazine, and hobbies. It is up to you to determine the actual field names and whether the database requires any additional fields. Once you arrive at a decision on a final field list, your next task is to group the fields to form three different tables. Since you are planning a relational database, the three tables must share a common field (most likely the identification number) so that they can be joined later. In the lessons that follow, you will learn how to construct a database and then enter its data. Of course, you must obtain the data first. As soon as you have established the design of your database by grouping the fields into three tables, gather the information necessary to complete records on the magazine preferences and profiles of 25 people.

Open the Microsoft Access Office Assistant. Ask him some questions and then read and learn about databases. Make sure you ask about all of the database objects including tables, queries, forms, and reports. Read anything that comes up along the way that you find interesting or that you think might come up later. This will give you a good background on the Lessons which are coming next.

Practice starting Access. Start Access and open some of the sample tables you find available. Search other folders and other locations on your desktop which might hold files or databases. Experiment with different ways to look in folders and open up files. Once you open a sample database, scroll through it. Look at the different types of data. Once you've viewed the databases used as samples make some changes. Try putting your name at the top or the bottom of the databases.

Once you have edited some of the material in the sample databases, print the database. First preview it and look at it in Page SetUp. Practice changing the dimensions of the pages. See what happens when you change the margins and the footers, and how it affects the way the databases will be printed on the screen.

L E S S O N

2

CREATING AND ARRANGING A DATABASE

As you have already learned, tables give a database its basic structure. After you create a new database in Access, the next step is to create the tables that store the database's data and fields. Creating a table in Design View allows you the greatest degree of control over the structure and functionality of a table. In Design View you can name fields, select their data types, add descriptive captions, and assign specific properties to the data in each field.

You enter and edit data in a table in Datasheet View. In this view, you can also make structural changes to a table like changing column width and field order. When you enter or edit data in Datasheet View, Access automatically saves the changes for you.

One of the greatest advantages of using database software is that you can arrange and rearrange the data you compile according to specific needs. Access provides a very versatile Find feature to locate specific data. You can also sort data, controlling the order in which records are displayed. Filters allow you to further control data by determining specific items which will be displayed.

You may also select specific data from a database by using a query. A query is a set of instructions which extracts certain pieces of information from tables. You can design, edit, and save a query for future use.

You may create relationships between tables to design queries that involve more than one table. You may link tables with a common field, linked tables can be queried as if they were one table.

CASE STUDY
In this lesson, Kyle will create a new database, and then design the database's primary table in Design View. He will also enter data in the table, edit it, and then save the table within the database. Finally, Kyle will make modifications to the design of his table in both Design View and Datasheet View.

Kyle will also use the find feature to locate a specific piece of information, and then he'll apply sorts and filters to his data. Later, he will design simple queries, and also design queries by linking tables in a relationship.

AC 2.1

Creating a New Database

Concept

In order to start working on a new database, you must first name it and save it.

Do It!

Kyle will now create and save a new database.

1 Open Access by clicking [Start], then clicking **Microsoft Access** on the Programs menu. The application will open with the Microsoft Access dialog box (**Figure 2-1**), asking whether you wish to create a new database or open an existing one.

2 Click the **Blank Database** radio button to select it, then click [OK]. The File New Database dialog box appears.

3 Click the **Save in** drop-down list arrow, then select your student disk or the drive where your Student Files folder is located. (Ask your instructor if you need further assistance.) This is where the new databases will be created.

4 With the Student Files folder showing in the Save in drop-down list box, click the **Create New Folder** button [icon] to open the New Folder dialog box.

5 Type **My Access Files**, as shown in **Figure 2-2**. Press [OK].

6 Once you create the **My Access Files** folder, its name will appear in the Save in drop-down list box, and the contents area will appear blank, indicating that the folder is empty. Your File New Database dialog box should now resemble the one shown in **Figure 2-3**.

Figure 2-1 Creating a new database

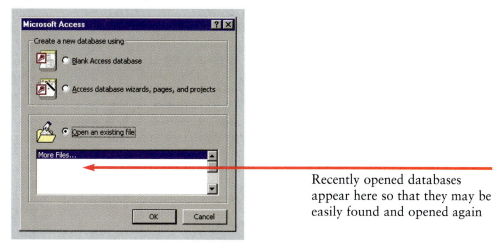

Recently opened databases
appear here so that they may be
easily found and opened again

Figure 2-2 New Folder dialog box

Enter a name here
for the folder that
is being created

Figure 2-3 File New Database dialog box

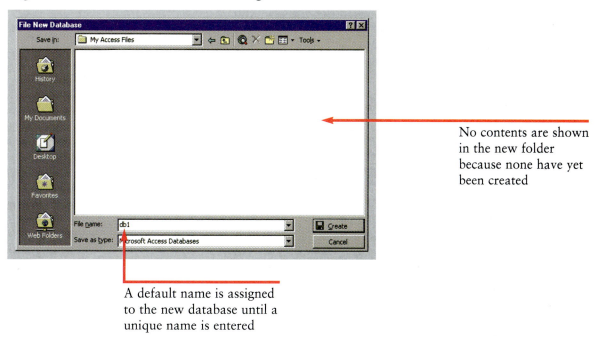

No contents are shown
in the new folder
because none have yet
been created

A default name is assigned
to the new database until a
unique name is entered

Creating a New Database (continued)

Do It!

7 Triple-click the File name: text box to select the contents of the text box, db1.mdb. Access assigns a default name to all newly created databases that consists of the letters db followed by a number, which is in turn followed by the file extension mdb. A file extension tells your computer what kind of information a file contains, and which applications may open it.

8 Type Employees. The text you enter will replace the selected default name. Access will automatically attach the .mdb file extension if you do not.

9 Click ⬚ Create ⬚. The dialog box disappears and a new Database window appears with the file name Employees in its title bar, as shown in **Figure 2-4**.

More

Another option to consider when creating a new database is the Database Wizard. Available on Access's opening screen, just below the Blank Database option, the Database Wizard brings up the Databases tab of the New dialog box, shown in **Figure 2-5**, which contains preconstructed database templates. Opening one of these templates activates the Wizard, which walks you through the steps of that database's construction. The Wizard is essentially an interface that asks you questions about the kinds of data your database will contain, as well as the way items in it will be displayed. When you have given it all the information it requests, it will create a database to meet the specifications that it has been given.

Figure 2-4 New database window

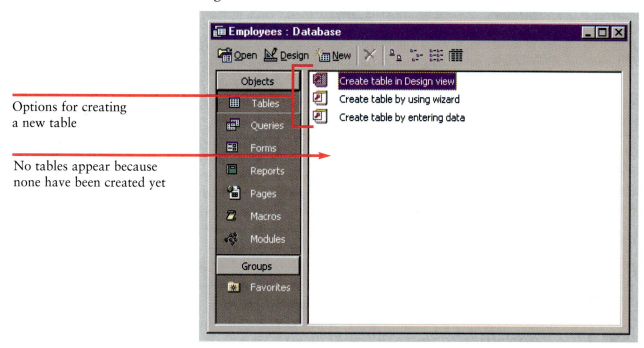

Options for creating
a new table

No tables appear because
none have been created yet

Figure 2-5 Database Wizards

This button is
depressed, indicating
that the Database
Wizards are shown
in List view

Practice

Open a second Access application window
by following the start procedures detailed
in Lesson 1, and create a new database
called **Inventory**. Save it in a new folder
named **My Practice Files** in the My Access
Files folder you created earlier in this Skill.

Hot Tip

If you are already working in Access and
wish to create a new database, use the
New Database button ▢ on the toolbar or
the corresponding command on the File
menu to bring up the New dialog box.

Creating a Table in Design View

Concept

A table is a collection of data about a specific topic that is organized into columns (called fields) and rows (called records). Using different tables for each topic ensures that data is stored only once, increasing database efficiency and decreasing the chance of mistakes. Creating a table in Design View allows you to define fields and assign properties to them. The Design View window is divided into two parts. The top section is a grid into which you enter the names of your fields, specify the type of data they hold, and enter descriptions that provide information about the field. The bottom section of the Design View window is the Field Properties pane, in which you may further define your fields' attributes.

Do It!

Kyle will use Design View to create a table in the new database.

1 Click [New] on the Tables tab of the Employees : Database window. The New Table dialog box, shown in **Figure 2-6**, and explained in **Table 2-1**, will appear on the screen.

2 Click Design View in the list box on the right side of the dialog box, to select it, then click [OK]. The Design View window opens with the insertion point in the first Field Name cell, and the Database toolbar changes to the Table Design toolbar. The status bar also changes, notifying you of Access' current mode.

3 Type Employee Number, then press [Enter]. The Data Type field now contains the highlighted word "Text," as well as a drop-down list arrow that allows you to choose from several data types that will constrain the kind of data that Access will accept as an entry for that field.

4 Press [Enter] to select the default data type, text, and move the insertion point to the Description field. Although the Number data type would suit the field, it does not allow an entry that has a zero at its beginning, and some employee numbers that will be entered in this field begin with a zero.

5 Type 3-digit number assigned consecutively to each employee as hired. This text will now appear in the status bar when any of the field's values are selected.

6 Double-click the Field Size text box on the General tab in the Field Properties section of the window to select the default field size, 50.

7 Press [3] to replace the default value with the number 3, limiting the maximum numbers of characters that may be entered into the field (see **Figure 2-7**).

8 Click the cell beneath the Employee Number in the Field Name column. The insertion point will move to the selected cell, and the field indicator arrow ▶ will move down to the second row, designating it as the active row.

9 Type Date Hired, then press [Enter] to move to the Data Type column.

10 Click the Data Type drop-down list arrow [▼], then select Date/Time from the list that appears to replace the default entry text. This instructs Access to accept only a date or a time in this field as a valid entry. This also alters the options available for modification on the General tab.

Table 2-1 Table Design Options

NEW TABLE OPTION	LETS YOU
Datasheet View	Begin entering and viewing your data right away, while Access automatically configures the table for you
Design View	Set the table's properties before you begin entering data
Table Wizard	Automate the task of table creation by asking questions about the information you wish to include in the database
Import Table	Use a table or object created at another time or in another application for use in a new database
Link Table	Create tables in the current database that are linked to tables in another file; changing the source table will alter the linked table in the Access database

Figure 2-6 New Table dialog box

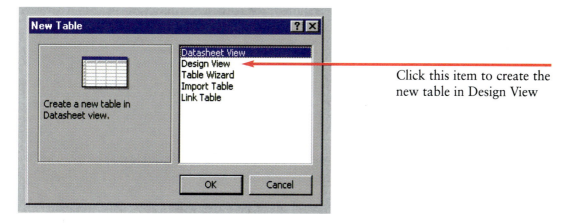

Click this item to create the new table in Design View

Figure 2-7 Creating a table in Design View

In Design View, each row pertains to a particular field in the table

Instructions and hints concerning the current field property appear here

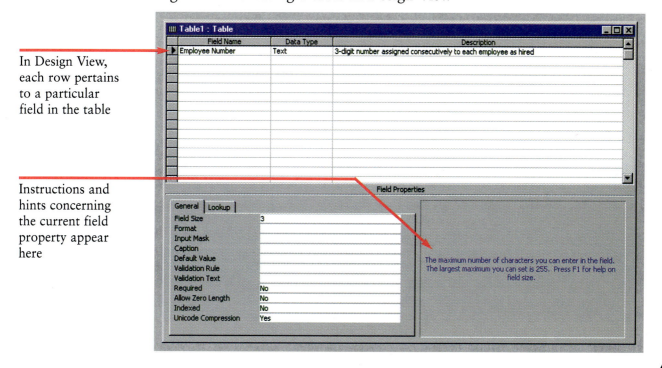

Creating a Table in Design View (continued)

Do It!

11 Click the Format text box on the General tab. An insertion point and a drop-down list arrow appear.

12 Click the drop-down list arrow in the Format text box and select Short Date from the list that appears, as shown in **Figure 2-8**. Short Date now appears in the Format text box as the selected format.

13 Click the Description cell in the Date Hired row to place the insertion point there, and type Acceptable entry formats are 6/13/98, Jun 13, 98, or June 13, 1998, then press [Enter]. The insertion point moves to the first cell in the next row.

14 Enter the following four field names into the next four rows, leaving the default setting of text in their Data Type fields, and leaving their Description fields blank: Last Name, First Name, Street, and City.

15 In the next blank Field Name cell, type State and press [Enter].

16 On the General tab, select the default Field Size of 50 and change it to 2, then press [Enter]. (This limits entries into this field to a two-letter state abbreviation.) The insertion point moves to the Format text box.

17 Type [>] ([Shift]+[.]) to place it in the Format text box. This character instructs Access to make all characters in this field uppercase, so that if someone were to enter ny, for example, it would appear as NY.

18 Click the Default Value text box on the General tab to place the insertion point there, then type NY. Since all of Stay Fast's employees live in New York, it is likely that NY would usually be entered in this field. With this default setting, NY will appear automatically in this field, but may be changed if necessary.

19 Click the Description field in the State row and type Default is NY; 2 character limit; converted to uppercase, then press [Enter].

20 Type Zip Code into the next blank Field Name field, leave the default text data type, and enter the description 10 character limit into the Description field.

21 Change the Field Size (on the General tab) to 10 to allow hyphenated zip codes.

22 Click the row selector button next to the Employee Number cell to select the entire row.

23 Click Edit, then click Primary Key. A small key icon will appear to the left of the field icon, as shown in **Figure 2-9**, indicating that the Employee Number field is now the primary key. The primary key field contains data that is common to every table in a database, which in this case will be the employee number. Primary key fields must be both unique and constant in order to guarantee a relationship between records in related tables. The three-digit employee number makes a good primary key field because it reflects the order in which an employee was hired, and is therefore both unique and constant. Do not close or alter this table, as it will be saved in the next Skill.

More

Notice that when the primary key is set, the Indexed property in the Field Properties area changes from No to Yes (No Duplicates). This prevents duplicate values from being entered in this field. Also, although the Required property does not reflect it, you must enter a value in a primary key field. This condition can also be applied to other fields by changing their Required property from No to Yes.

Database tables need not share the same primary key fields. For example, the Employee Number field may be the primary key field in one table, such as a basic employee roster, but in a related table that lists account managers and the clients that they are responsible for, an employee's number may be linked to more than one client. In that case, an employee's number could occur more than once in a table and would be disallowed as a primary key. Employee Number would still function as a common field, however, and would allow you to link the two tables. In such a situation, employee number is called a foreign key field.

Figure 2-8 Choosing a Date/Time format

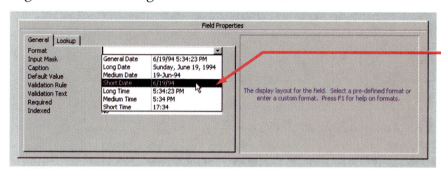

The date or time format is illustrated in the right half of the drop-down list

Access 2000

Figure 2-9 Setting the primary key

The data appearing in the field marked by the primary key symbol appears in every table in the database

New Access 2000 feature which provides a more efficient way to save your table

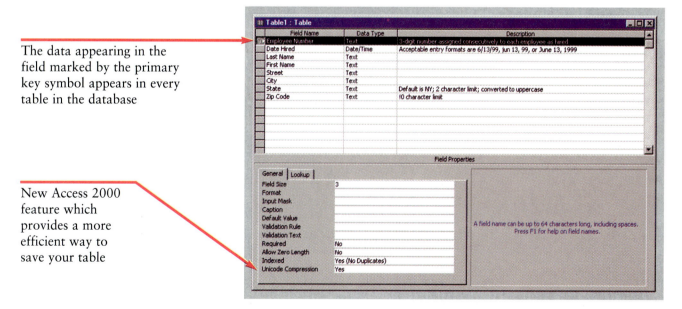

Practice

Create a table that includes the following fields, in this order: **Item #**, **To Be Ordered**, **Product**, **Price**, and **Quantity on Hand**. Include appropriate data type formatting and descriptions, and make Item # the primary key field.

Hot Tip

The Lookup tab of the Field Properties section lets you make list boxes or combo list/text boxes out of your fields. This would allow you to create a list box, for example, that would let you choose from a list of cities instead of typing one manually.

Saving and Viewing a Table

Concept

Once a table is created it must be saved to a disk so that the information can be retrieved later for viewing or editing. If you do not save your work it will be lost when the application it was created in is exited. It is a good idea to save frequently so as not to lose any data due to computer failure.

Do It!

Kyle will save the table that has been created and then view it in Datasheet View.

1 Click File, then click Save As... The Save As dialog box, pictured in **Figure 2-10**, comes up with the contents of the current database text box selected for editing.

2 Type Employee Roster to replace the default table name, Table1.

3 Click OK. The Save As dialog box closes, the table is saved within the open Employees database, and the table name Employee Roster is displayed in the title bar of the Design View window.

4 Click the View button to go to Datasheet View. The table appears reconfigured with the previously defined field names as column headings, as seen in **Figure 2-11**. These columns intersect with rows to form the field cells into which you will enter data. A single row of this table comprises a record, which is all the data relating to a single item. (In this case, each employee.)

5 Click the Save button to save your database.

More

The two table views serve different purposes. In Design View, you set up the table's structure so that it can accept data in specific ways. Data does not appear in Design View, but can be seen, entered, and edited in Datasheet View, where all of the field formats and restrictions that you set in Design View apply.

Figure 2-11 shows the Datasheet View window with one blank record. To the left of the record is a gray button know as the Record Selector button. The right-pointing arrow on this button indicates which record is currently active. At the bottom of the window is the Specific Record box, which displays the number of the record you are currently working on. The buttons to either side of the Specific Record box are for navigating between records in the table.

Figure 2-10 Save As dialog box for tables

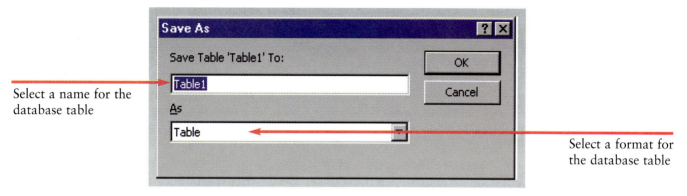

Select a name for the
database table

Select a format for
the database table

Figure 2-11 Appearance of the new table

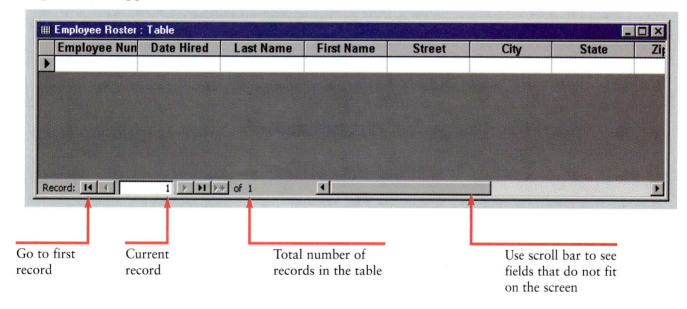

Go to first
record

Current
record

Total number of
records in the table

Use scroll bar to see
fields that do not fit
on the screen

Save the table you created in the previous
Practice, naming it **Orders**. Then, display
the table in **Datasheet View**.

Hot Tip

The View button toggles between Design
and Datasheet Views, but you cannot
switch to Datasheet View until the table's
design has been saved.

 # Entering Data in a Table

Concept

Once a table's fields have been defined, you may start entering data in the form of records. Each record, or row of data in the table, contains the information specific to one item or individual. The more carefully you have planned and designed your table, the easier and quicker this phase of database construction will be.

Do It!

Kyle is now ready to begin entering data into the table he has created.

1. Type 001 into the Employee Number field, then press [Enter]. Notice that as soon as a character is typed, the Record Selector arrow ▶ changes to a pencil ✐ to indicate that the record is being edited (see **Table 2-2**). Also, a second blank record appears beneath the first with an asterisk ✳ in its Record Selector button, which indicates that this is currently the last record in the table. The insertion point moves to the Date Hired field and the description you entered earlier appears in the status bar.

2. Type June 5, 1993 and press [Enter]. The insertion point will move to the Last Name field, and the date you entered will be converted to a shorter form due to the settings in its field properties.

3. Type Busing, press [Enter], type Klaus, press [Enter], and then type 112 Memorial Dr. to place the names and address into their proper fields. The street address you entered does not fit into the Street field in its entirety; the field's width will be adjusted in a later Skill. Likewise, some field names do not fit into their cells. This too will be remedied later on.

4. Type Irvington, then press [Enter] twice, since the correct entry, NY, is already present in the State field. The insertion point moves into the Zip Code field.

5. Type 10533, then press [Enter]. The insertion point moves to the first field of the next record.

6. Enter the following record into the appropriate fields, as you did above: 002, June 5, 1993, Young, Tracy, 665 Boylston St., Elmsford, NY, 10523. Your table should now resemble **Figure 2-12**.

7. Click Window, then click Employees: Database to activate the Database window and bring it to the front. The menu bar and toolbar also change to reflect the active window.

8. Click the Database window's Close button ⊠. Both the Database window and the Table window close.

More

When you closed the Database window, Access did not prompt you to save any changes that you had made. This is because changes made to data are saved as they are entered, while changes to a table's structure or attributes (like those made in Design View) must be manually saved to take effect.

Table 2-2 Record Selectors

ICON	INDICATES
▶	Current record; the record has been saved as it appears
✻	A new record that you can add to
🖉	A record that is being edited, and whose changes have not yet been saved
⊘	A record that has been locked by another user, and that cannot be edited

Figure 2-12   Entering records in a table

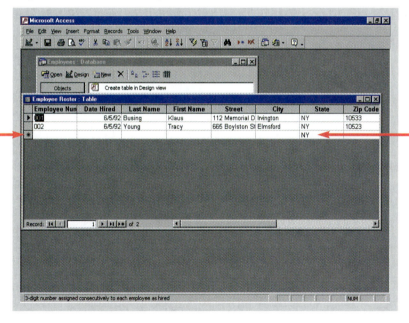

Denotes currently active record

The State field already contains a value because one was specified earlier in its field properties

Practice

Obtain a mail-order catalog. Select ten items and enter their product information into the appropriate fields in your Orders table. Save the table when you are done.

Hot Tip

Pressing [Tab], like pressing [Enter], moves the insertion point to the next field in a record.

 **Using the Export Command**

Concept

The Export command allows you to save a database in a new location. You must first create a blank database into which you can export database objects in order to save it in this new location.

Do It!

Kyle must create a new database so that he can save the database he has created in a new location.

1 Click the New button ▢ on the toolbar to open the New dialog box.

2 Click 〔 OK 〕 to select the default Blank Database. The File New Database dialog box appears.

3 Locate the My Access Files folder that you created earlier to store your databases and double-click it to open it. It will appear in the Save in drop-down list box, and its contents will be listed below, as shown in **Figure 2-13**.

4 Triple-click the File name text box to highlight its contents.

5 Type Employees 2 and click 〔 Create 〕. A Database window opens for the new database, Employees 2.

6 Click the Open button 📂 on the toolbar to bring up the Open dialog box, then select the student file Doit2-5. It is located in the Student Files folder.

7 Click 〔 Open 〕. The database that opens is the one you created, but with more records added. Since Access can only support one open database at a time, the new database you created closes.

8 Click File, then click Export.

9 Locate and select the Employees 2 database that you just created in the Student Files folder, then click Save All. The Export dialog box, pictured in **Figure 2-14**, appears with the default table name, Employee Roster, in the Export Employee Roster to text box.

10 Click 〔 OK 〕. The data is exported to the target file.

More

Access will only allow you to export one database object at a time. Since the database you were using contained only one object, this was not an issue. However, if you wish to export several objects at once, you must open the target database and then use the Import command on the Get External data submenu of the File menu. After selecting the database from which you will be importing objects, a Database window will appear, on which you may select the objects you wish to import.

Sometimes you may wish to use a table you have created with different data and for a different purpose. To export just the structure of a table so that you may use it as a template in this fashion, simply click the Definition Only radio button on the Export dialog box when exporting the table.

Figure 2-13 File New Database dialog box

Figure 2-14 Export dialog box

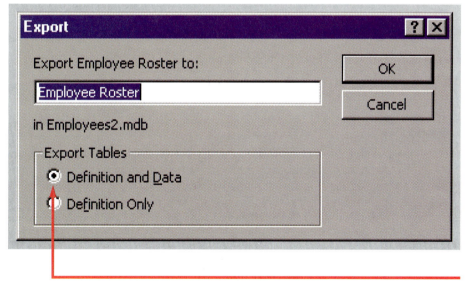

Exports both the table's design
information and the table's data

To practice exporting database objects create a new database in your My Practice
Files folder called Inventory 2, then export
the Orders table to the new database.

Hot Tip

If you wish to open more than one database at a time, you can open it with another copy of the Access application. Open
Access as you normally would, whether
from an icon on the desktop or from the
Start menu, then open the target database.

Editing Information in a Table

Concept

Data that has been entered into a table can be easily modified to reflect changes or correct mistakes.

Do It!

Kyle must open the new database and then fix a typing error that he made when he was adding records to the table.

1 Click the Open button 📂 on the toolbar to bring up the Open dialog box, then select the Employees 2 database that you created in the previous Skill, which should be located in the My Access Files folder.

2 Click [Open] to open the selected database and close Doit2-5.

3 Double-click the Employee Roster table, shown on the Tables tab of the Database window, to open it. The table opens with records for fifty employees showing.

4 Scroll down to the record for employee 020. Carolyn's last name was misspelled, and must be corrected.

5 Move the mouse pointer, which is now an I-beam Ⅰ, between the ; and the g, as shown in **Figure 2-15**, and click once to place the insertion point there.

6 Press [Back Space] to delete the semicolon, then press [←]. The insertion point skips to the left one character.

7 Press [Back Space] again to delete the zero, then press [o] to correct the name so that it is spelled Wong, as shown in **Figure 2-16**.

More

The Undo button 🔙 on the toolbar lets you take back changes you have made to a record. Clicking it once undoes the last change made, such as a single keystroke. Clicking it again will undo changes made to the field. Clicking the Undo button a third time will revert the entire record to the form in which it was last saved. It is important that you remember that once you begin editing another record or switch to another window, the changes you have made are saved and cannot be undone.

Access also contains a spell-checking facility, which can be used to selectively search for spelling errors in database objects such as tables, forms, and queries. The Spelling dialog box, accessible by clicking the Spelling button 🔤 or by its menu command on the tools menu, is shown in **Figure 2-17**. It searches for words not contained within its dictionary and brings them to your attention. If the spelling checker stops on a word that it does not recognize, but that you know is correct, you may click [Add] to add the selected word to Access' custom dictionary, which is a document containing all words that are added in this fashion. Access will consult this document on future occasions when running the spelling checker, and will no longer stop on these words. If you do not wish to add the selected word to the custom dictionary, click [Ignore] to go to the next word without changing it, or [Ignore All] to ignore all instances of the word in the document. Access' spelling checker also allows you to skip entire fields, such as a name or street field, that are sure to contain many words that it will not recognize.

Figure 2-15 Employee Roster table with all records entered

Employee Num	Date Hired	Last Name	First Name	Street	City	State	
013	8/21/94	Lee	Mike	72 Charles St	Dobbs Ferry	NY	10!
014	8/23/94	Abdo	Muhammad	112 Atlantic Ave	Scarsdale	NY	10!
015	9/24/94	Reynolds	Ken	25 Flute Pl	Scarsdale	NY	10!
016	9/25/94	Collins	Elmer	17 Cornell Ave	Elmsford	NY	10!
017	12/17/94	Harris	Lorna	43 Lindy Dr	Hartsdale	NY	10!
018	3/4/95	Nowak	Jasmine	39 Davis Ave	Briarcliff Manor	NY	10!
019	4/19/95	Rosafort	Lyle	1 Upland Ln	Elmsford	NY	10!
020	4/25/95	WOn;g	Carolyn	12 Spiff St	Valhalla	NY	10!
021	6/3/95	Johnson	John	345 White Ave	Scarsdale	NY	10!
022	6/6/95	Wolff	Henryk	204 Hamilton R(	Chappaqua	NY	10!

Record: ◄◄ ◄ 20 ► ►◄ ►* of 50

Place the I-beam here to correct the mistake

Figure 2-16 Editing information in a table

Employee Num	Date Hired	Last Name	First Name	Street	City	State	
013	8/21/94	Lee	Mike	72 Charles St	Dobbs Ferry	NY	10!
014	8/23/94	Abdo	Muhammad	112 Atlantic Ave	Scarsdale	NY	10!
015	9/24/94	Reynolds	Ken	25 Flute Pl	Scarsdale	NY	10!
016	9/25/94	Collins	Elmer	17 Cornell Ave	Elmsford	NY	10!
017	12/17/94	Harris	Lorna	43 Lindy Dr	Hartsdale	NY	10!
018	3/4/95	Nowak	Jasmine	39 Davis Ave	Briarcliff Manor	NY	10!
019	4/19/95	Rosafort	Lyle	1 Upland Ln	Elmsford	NY	10!
020	4/25/95	Wong	Carolyn	12 Spiff St	Valhalla	NY	10!
021	6/3/95	Johnson	John	345 White Ave	Scarsdale	NY	10!
022	6/6/95	Wolff	Henryk	204 Hamilton R(	Chappaqua	NY	10!

Record: ◄◄ ◄ 20 ► ►◄ ►* of 50

Correct spelling of Carolyn's last name

Figure 2-17 Spelling dialog box

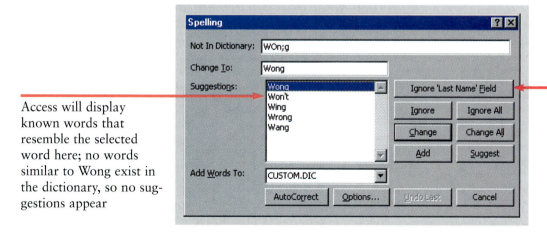

Access will display known words that resemble the selected word here; no words similar to Wong exist in the dictionary, so no suggestions appear

Click to disregard unrecognized words in the specified field

Practice

Change two of the quantities in the To Be Ordered field. Then, spell check your table for any typing errors you may have made. Finally, fix any mistakes that are found.

Hot Tip

If you need to delete an entire record, first click in any of its fields, then use either the Delete Record command on the Edit menu, or the corresponding button ▣ on the toolbar. Once you delete a record, it cannot be retrieved.

Manipulating Column Widths

Concept

By default, fields in a table are displayed in a cell that is approximately one inch wide, regardless of its content. Sometimes, this can be too wide, wasting space on the screen. In other cases, a cell may be too narrow, obscuring some of the field data. You can adjust the width of columns so as to reduce wasted screen space and maximize the amount of data that can be seen on the screen at one time.

Do It!

Kyle would like to adjust the width of several of his columns so that they present their data more effectively in his table.

1. Move the mouse pointer to the border between the Employee Number and Date Hired field names. The pointer will change to the resizing pointer ↔, indicating that the boundary can be moved.

2. Using the resizing pointer, click and drag the column boundary to the right until the entire field name, Employee Number, is visible. A black vertical line indicates where the new boundary will appear when the mouse button is released.

3. Click the Date Hired field selector button (the gray box in which the words Date Hired appear) to select the entire column.

4. Click the Zip Code field selector button while pressing [Shift]. All columns from Date Hired to Zip Code will be selected, as shown in **Figure 2-18**. You may have to use the horizontal scroll bar to see the Zip Code field.

5. Click Format, then click Column Width. The Column Width dialog box, shown in **Figure 2-19**, appears with the column width selected.

6. Click Best Fit . Each of the selected columns expands or contracts so that it is just wide enough to contain the largest field in the column.

7. Click once anywhere in the table to deselect the highlighted columns. Your table should look like the one in **Figure 2-20**.

More

You may determine the width of columns in several ways. The Column Width dialog box lets you automatically adjust the width of the selected column(s) by using the Best Fit button, or you can manually enter a column width into the Column Width text box. Once a column's width has been changed, you may make it revert to the default column width by checking the Standard Width check box.

The height of a table's rows may be adjusted in much the same way that its columns are. The Row Height dialog box, available on the Format menu, lets you manually set the height of all rows in a table, or revert to the standard height. The standard height is based on the font size being used in the table. You may also adjust the height of a table's rows by clicking the border between row selector buttons and dragging up or down. The pointer will change to a vertical resizing pointer, and a horizontal black line will indicate where the new boundary will appear when the mouse button is released. Though you may make a row any height you wish, all rows in a table will have the same height.

Figure 2-18 Selecting multiple columns

Several columns may be selected at the same time so that they may be acted upon as a unit

Figure 2-19 Column Width dialog box

Applies the default column width (approximately one screen inch) to the selected columns

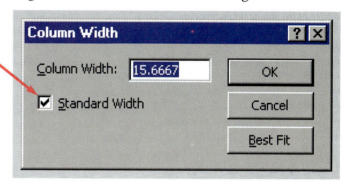

Figure 2-20 Table with adjusted column widths

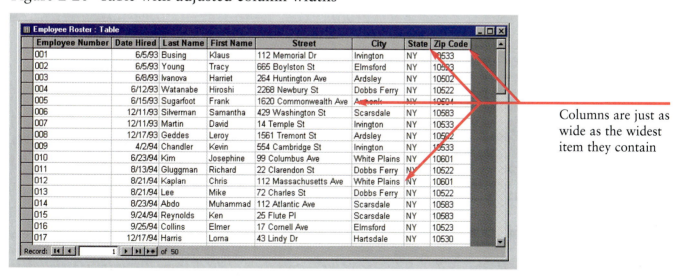

Columns are just as wide as the widest item they contain

Practice

Adjust all of the columns so that they are the optimum width for the data they contain.

Hot Tip

Double-clicking the boundary between field selector buttons with the resizing pointer will automatically adjust the width of the column on the left to its optimum width, just as the Best Fit button adjusts the width of all selected columns.

Editing and Arranging Fields

Concept

At times, you may wish to change the names of fields to more accurately describe the information they contain or to better fit them into an appropriate column width. Access not only lets you easily rename fields, but also allows you to move and reposition them.

Do It!

Kyle will rename some of his fields so that they take up less space, and will move the First Name field so that it comes before Last Name.

1. Place the insertion point in the Employee Number column, then click Format, followed by Rename Column. The field name will appear highlighted, with a blinking insertion point positioned at its beginning.

2. Type Employee # to replace the previous name, then press [Enter] to save the change.

3. Follow the previous steps to change the Date Hired field name to Hired, and to change Zip Code to Zip.

4. Double-click the right edges of the Employee #, Hired, and Zip field selector buttons with the resizing pointer to automatically fit the columns into the least amount of space without obscuring any of their contents.

5. Click the First Name field selector button to select the entire column.

6. Click and drag the First Name field selector button to the left until a vertical black line appears between Hired and Last Name fields, then release the mouse button. The entire column moves to the new location, effectively causing the First Name and Last Name fields to trade positions. Your table should now look like the one shown in **Figure 2-21**.

More

The Format menu contains commands that affect the way in which table elements appear on the screen. The Font command brings up the Font dialog box, which controls such text aspects as font and font size, style, color, and effects. The Hide Columns command does just what it says, allowing you to hide a column from view while still letting you include its contents as sorting and filtering criteria. The Unhide Columns command opens a dialog box, shown in **Figure 2-22**, which displays a check box for each of your fields; checking a box will make its corresponding column visible, while unchecking the box will hide the column from view. Finally, the Freeze Columns command lets you freeze one or more columns on a datasheet so that they become the leftmost columns of your table. These columns will be visible at all times, no mater where you scroll. This is especially useful in very wide tables, where it may be difficult to match up data in two columns that are too far apart to be viewed simultaneously.

Figure 2-21 Renamed and rearranged fields in a table

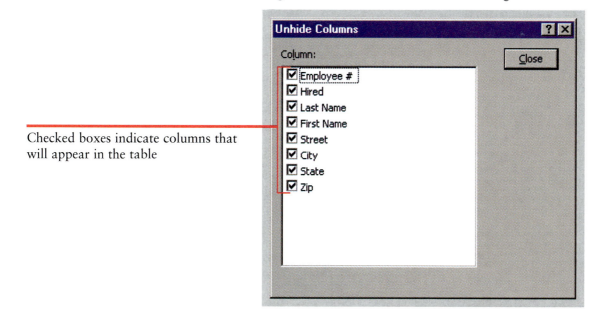

Employee #	Hired	Last Name	First Name	Street	City	State	Zip
001	6/5/93	Busing	Klaus	112 Memorial Dr	Irvington	NY	10533
002	6/5/93	Young	Tracy	665 Boylston St	Elmsford	NY	10523
003	6/8/93	Ivanova	Harriet	264 Huntington Ave	Ardsley	NY	10502
004	6/12/93	Watanabe	Hiroshi	2268 Newbury St	Dobbs Ferry	NY	10522
005	6/15/93	Sugarfoot	Frank	1620 Commonwealth Ave	Armonk	NY	10504
006	12/11/93	Silverman	Samantha	429 Washington St	Scarsdale	NY	10583
007	12/11/93	Martin	David	14 Temple St	Irvington	NY	10533
008	12/17/93	Geddes	Leroy	1561 Tremont St	Ardsley	NY	10502
009	4/2/94	Chandler	Kevin	554 Cambridge St	Irvington	NY	10533
010	6/23/94	Kim	Josephine	99 Columbus Ave	White Plains	NY	10601
011	8/13/94	Gluggman	Richard	22 Clarendon St	Dobbs Ferry	NY	10522
012	8/21/94	Kaplan	Chris	112 Massachusetts Ave	White Plains	NY	10601
013	8/21/94	Lee	Mike	72 Charles St	Dobbs Ferry	NY	10522
014	8/23/94	Abdo	Muhammad	112 Atlantic Ave	Scarsdale	NY	10583
015	9/24/94	Reynolds	Ken	25 Flute Pl	Scarsdale	NY	10583
016	9/25/94	Collins	Elmer	17 Cornell Ave	Elmsford	NY	10523
017	12/17/94	Harris	Lorna	43 Lindy Dr	Hartsdale	NY	10530

Record: 1 of 50

Figure 2-22 Unhide Columns dialog box

Checked boxes indicate columns that will appear in the table

Practice

Rename the To Be Ordered column so it reads Number Needed. Then, move the Number Needed column so that it is the last in the table.

Hot Tip

Double-clicking a field selector button selects it for modification, just as it does when using the Rename Column command on the Format menu.

Adding a Field

Concept

Once a table has been created, fields may still be added or removed at any time. While fields may be added in Datasheet View, Design View offers much more control over the properties of your fields.

Do It!

Kyle wants to add a new field to his table, and to set its properties so as to restrict the data that may be entered into the field.

1 Click the View button on the toolbar to toggle to Design View.

2 Click the empty cell below the Zip field to place the insertion point there.

3 Type Gender, then press [Enter]. The Data Type field becomes selected.

4 Double-click the Field Size text box on the General tab of the Field Properties section to select the default value of 50.

5 Type 1, then press [Enter]. The insertion point moves to the Format field property.

6 Type > ([Shift]+[.]). Access will make all contents of this field appear in uppercase.

7 Click in the Validation Rule text box to place the insertion point there.

8 Type ="M" Or "F" to set the validation rule. When you set a validation rule, Access checks all entries in the field against the rule. Entries that do not fall within the bounds of the rule are not accepted.

9 Click in the Validation Text text box to place the insertion point there, then type You may enter only M or F. This is the error message that will be displayed if a value other than M or F is entered into this field. Your table should resemble the one shown in **Figure 2-23**.

10 Click the Save button to save the design changes you have made. A dialog box, shown in **Figure 2-24** will appear asking whether you want to test existing data under the new rule.

11 Since this is a new field and there is no existing data, click No. The dialog box disappears, and the table is saved with the changes you have made.

12 Click the Close buttons on the Design View and Database windows to close the file.

More

In the example above, the new field was added to the end of the table. New fields may also be inserted into the middle of a table by using the Rows command on the Insert menu in Design View. A new row will be added above the row in which the insertion point currently resides. New fields may also be added in Datasheet View using the Columns command on the Insert menu, but Datasheet View does not offer the kind of control over field properties that is available in Design View. Commands are available on the Edit menu in both views to delete selected fields.

Figure 2-23 Adding a field to a table in Design View

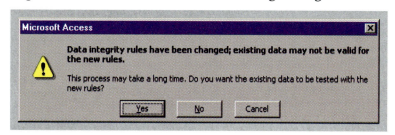

The validation
text appears if
the validation
rule is not met

Figure 2-24 Microsoft Access warning dialog box

Practice

Add a field called Additional Information with its description reading: color, size, variety, etc. Then close the database and the application, saving changes if you are prompted to do so.

Hot Tip

In Design View, you may add or remove selected rows in the table by using the Insert Rows button  or the Delete Rows button on the toolbar.

Importing Database Objects

Concept

You may easily import objects from other databases into the open database.

Do It!

Kyle wants to create a new database and then import several objects into it from another database.

1 Click the New button ⬜ to open the New dialog box.

2 Click ⬜ OK to accept the default Blank Database. The File New Database dialog box will open.

3 Create a new database called Employees 3 and save it in the My Access Files folder within your Student Files folder. When it has been created, the dialog box will close and the Database window will appear on the screen.

4 Click File, then select Import from the Get External Data submenu. The Import dialog box will open, as shown in **Figure 2-25**.

5 Locate and select the student file Doit2-10, which should be located in your Student Files folder.

6 Click ⬜ Import . The Import Objects dialog box, shown in **Figure 2-26**, appears with the selected database's window showing. This will let you choose the objects that you wish to import.

7 Click ⬜ Select All to select all available database objects, then click ⬜ OK . Access will import the selected objects into the Employees 3 database and close the Import Objects dialog box.

More

The Office Links submenu of the Tools menu offers commands that can link your database to other Microsoft Office files. A common use for the Merge It with MS Word command on this submenu is the creation of Mail Merge documents using Microsoft Word as the editor and an Access database as the datasheet. This could enable you to create a form letter in Word, for example, and to print out as many copies as you wish, each personalized with information drawn from the Access employees table that you have created, with names, addresses, and other information automatically inserted into their proper places in each letter.

You may also use Microsoft Word to view a datasheet by using the Publish It with MS Word command on the Office Links submenu. This allows you to create Word documents containing partial or whole database objects. Using this command will open Word and display the selected database as an rtf (Rich Text Format) file, which is a text format that maintains formatting information.

Access offers a similar link to Excel, using the Analyze It with MS Excel command, that lets you open databases as Excel files so that Excel's analytical, computational, and display features may be fully utilized.

Figure 2-25 Import dialog box

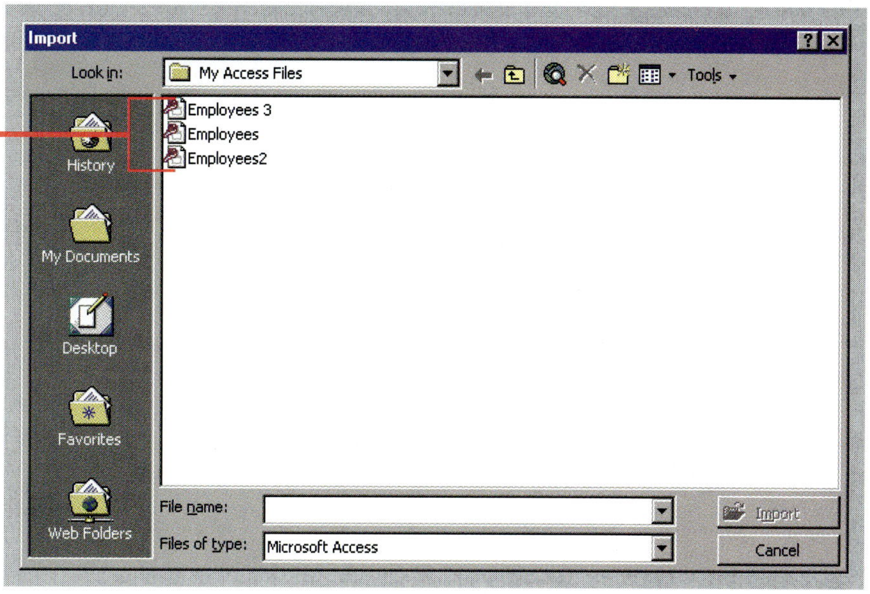

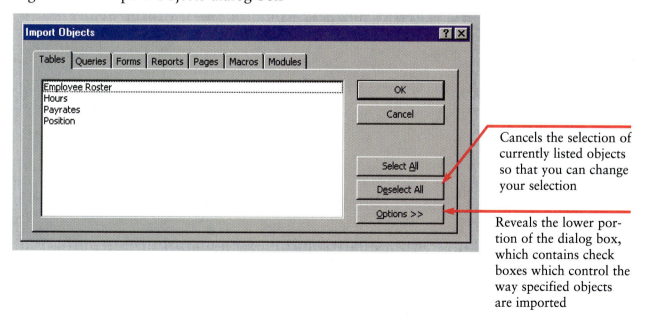

Objects may be import-
ed from any of these
databases

Figure 2-26 Import Objects dialog box

Cancels the selection of
currently listed objects
so that you can change
your selection

Reveals the lower por-
tion of the dialog box,
which contains check
boxes which control the
way specified objects
are imported

Practice

Open another Access application window,
as you did for the practice file in the previous Lesson. Then create a new database
called **Tuning Tracker** and import the two
tables from practice 2-12

Hot Tip

The Office Links button and list arrow
available on the toolbar when the Database
window is active, provides another way to
get to the Office Link commands.

Finding Information in a Table

Concept

Access contains a wide variety of powerful search features that enable you to find the information you are looking for in your tables quickly and accurately.

Do It!

One of Stay Fast's employees, Laura Van Pelt, has married another employee. Kyle will use Access' search capabilities to quickly find the record so that her name and address information may be updated.

1 Double-click the Employee Roster table icon on the Tables tab of the Database window to open it in Datasheet View.

2 Click the Last Name field selector button to select the entire column.

3 Click Edit, then click Find to open the Find and Replace dialog box, which is pictured in **Figure 2-27**. Notice that it will search only within the previously selected field.

4 Type Van Pelt into the Find What text box, then click Find Next. Access searches for the words Van Pelt in the Last Name fields, and scrolls down to show the selected field.

5 Close the Find and Replace dialog box.

6 Type Geddes to replace Van Pelt with Laura's new last name.

7 Press [Tab] twice to select the Street field in Laura's record, then type in her new address to replace it, 1561 Tremont St.

8 Press [Tab] to go to the City field, then type Ardsley to replace the previous city.

9 Press [Tab] twice to select the Zip field, then type 10502.

More

Access can still search for items in a table if only a fragment is known. If you had typed De into the Find in field : "Last Name" dialog box and selected Start of Field in the Match drop-down list, Access would have come up with the record for DeBois. If the Match drop-down list was set to Any Part of Field, Access would also find Geddes, Adelman, and McBride, since these contain the "de" sequence in places other than the beginning of the field. The Whole Field option in the Match drop-down list instructs Access to search for fields that contain only what is shown in the Find What text box. In this case, it would only find a field if the field contained "de" and nothing else. If the Match drop-down list box were set to anything other than Whole Field and the Match Case check box were checked, Access would find only DeBois, since the combination of uppercase and lowercase letters in the Find What check box match those in DeBois. As you can see, these options may be used individually or in combination to fine tune your search efforts.

Table 2-3 Search Parameter Wildcard Characters

WILDCARD	USED FOR	EXAMPLE
*	Matching any number of characters; may be placed at the beginning, end, or in the middle of text	thr* finds throw, through, and thrush
?	Matching any single alphabetic character	t?n finds tan, ten, and tin, but not town
[ ]	Matching any single character within the brackets	t[ae]n finds tan and ten, but not tin
[!]	Matching any character not in the brackets	t[!ae] finds tin and ton, but not tan or ten
[-]	Matching any one of a range of characters, specified in alphabetical order	ta[a-m] will find tab and tag, but not tan or tap
#	Matching any single numeric character	4#0 will find 410 and 420, but not 4110 or 415

Access 2000

Figure 2-27 Find and Replace dialog box

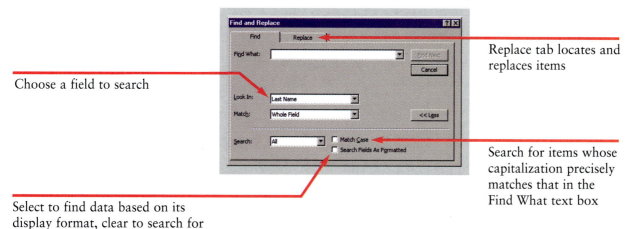

Replace tab locates and replaces items

Choose a field to search

Search for items whose capitalization precisely matches that in the Find What text box

Select to find data based on its display format, clear to search for data based on its value; searching by format is usually slowest

Practice

Use the Access Find feature to search the Customers table in the Tuning Tracker database for the person who lives on 38th Street.

Hot Tip

The Replace tab on the dialog box shown above is like the Find tab, but contains a Replace With text box that allows you to automatically replace items throughout the table with an entry that you specify.

Filtering and Sorting Records in a Table

Concept

Access allows you to use several filtering and sorting criteria to organize the records in your tables. Filters control what items are shown, while sorting determines the order in which they are displayed.

Do It!

Kyle wants to display the records for the employees that live in Elmsford.

1. Click anywhere in the City field. By default, the Sort feature will sort the field which holds the insertion point.

2. Click the Sort Ascending button 🔼 on the toolbar. The records are displayed in a new order, listing employees by their cities of residence from Ardsley to White Plains. Now all employees from Elmsford are grouped together in the table, as shown in **Figure 2-28**.

3. Since only those records belonging to employees who live in Elmsford are needed, click one of the Elmsford fields to place the insertion point there. This will select the contents of the field for filtering purposes.

4. Click the Filter By Selection button 🔽 on the toolbar. Access filters the table based on the contents of the selected field, the Apply Filter button on the toolbar becomes depressed and changes to the Remove Filter button, and only the records for employees living in Elmsford are displayed, as you can see in **Figure 2-29**. Now you will return the table to its original form.

5. Click the Remove Filter button 🔽 to show all records.

6. Click the Employee # field, then click the Sort Ascending button to sort the records in order of increasing Employee #.

7. Close the table, saving changes if prompted to do so.

More

Unlike the Filter By Selection command, the Filter Excluding Selection command (which has no button on the toolbar by default, but is located with the other filter commands on the Records menu) will display all records in the table that do **not** contain the specified field contents.

The Filter By Form Command displays the Filter By Form window in place of your Datasheet View. In this window, you may select several filter criteria from the fields in your table, and you may even use more than one entry for a single field by using the Or tabs at the bottom of the window. For example, you can view just the records of the female employees living in Irvington by selecting those criteria in their respective fields in the Filter By Form window. To display all female employees who live in both Irvington and Dobbs Ferry, you would select the same criteria as before, then click the Or tab, which allows you to select Dobbs Ferry as a second filtering criterion in the City field.

Figure 2-28 Table sorted in ascending order by City

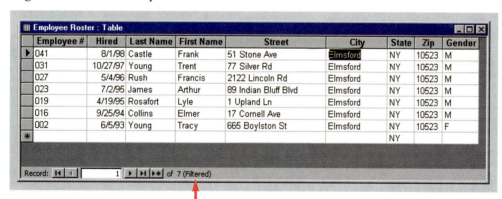

Employee #	Hired	Last Name	First Name	Street	City	State	Zip	Gender
003	6/8/93	Ivanova	Harriet	264 Huntington Ave	Ardsley	NY	10502	F
050	6/5/99	Geddes	Laura	1561 Tremont St	Ardsley	NY	10502	F
008	12/17/93	Geddes	Leroy	1561 Tremont St	Ardsley	NY	10502	M
005	6/15/93	Sugarfoot	Frank	1620 Commonwealth Ave	Armonk	NY	10504	M
018	3/4/95	Nowak	Jasmine	39 Davis Ave	Briarcliff Manor	NY	10510	F
033	1/2/98	Collins	John	449 Roaring Brook Blvd	Briarcliff Manor	NY	10510	M
045	12/15/98	DeBois	Kirby	25 Springfield Ln	Bronxville	NY	10708	M
022	6/6/95	Wolff	Henryk	204 Hamilton Rd	Chappaqua	NY	10514	M
011	8/13/94	Gluggman	Richard	22 Clarendon St	Dobbs Ferry	NY	10522	M
029	5/11/96	Smith	Rhonda	11 Smith Ave	Dobbs Ferry	NY	10522	F
032	1/2/98	McDonald	John	76 Smith Ave	Dobbs Ferry	NY	10522	M
013	8/21/94	Lee	Mike	72 Charles St	Dobbs Ferry	NY	10522	M
004	6/12/93	Watanabe	Hiroshi	2268 Newbury St	Dobbs Ferry	NY	10522	M
040	7/3/98	Lee	Mike	9 Livingston Pl	Eastchester	NY	10709	M
037	4/21/98	Prakash	Dom	7 Garden Pl	Eastchester	NY	10709	M
031	10/27/97	Young	Trent	77 Silver Rd	Elmsford	NY	10523	M
002	6/5/93	Young	Tracy	665 Boylston St	Elmsford	NY	10523	F
019	4/19/95	Rosafort	Lyle	1 Upland Ln	Elmsford	NY	10523	M
023	7/2/95	James	Arthur	89 Indian Bluff Blvd	Elmsford	NY	10523	M
016	9/25/94	Collins	Elmer	17 Cornell Ave	Elmsford	NY	10523	M
041	8/1/98	Castle	Frank	51 Stone Ave	Elmsford	NY	10523	M
027	5/4/96	Rush	Francis	2122 Lincoln Rd	Elmsford	NY	10523	M
017	12/17/94	Harris	Lorna	43 Lindy Dr	Hartsdale	NY	10530	F

Record: 1 of 50

The desired records are now grouped together because of the sorting criterion that was imposed

Figure 2-29 Filter by Selection

Employee #	Hired	Last Name	First Name	Street	City	State	Zip	Gender
041	8/1/98	Castle	Frank	51 Stone Ave	Elmsford	NY	10523	M
031	10/27/97	Young	Trent	77 Silver Rd	Elmsford	NY	10523	M
027	5/4/96	Rush	Francis	2122 Lincoln Rd	Elmsford	NY	10523	M
023	7/2/95	James	Arthur	89 Indian Bluff Blvd	Elmsford	NY	10523	M
019	4/19/95	Rosafort	Lyle	1 Upland Ln	Elmsford	NY	10523	M
016	9/25/94	Collins	Elmer	17 Cornell Ave	Elmsford	NY	10523	M
002	6/5/93	Young	Tracy	665 Boylston St	Elmsford	NY	10523	F
*						NY		

Record: 1 of 7 (Filtered)

Indicates that the entire table is not displayed

Practice

Sort the Customers table of the Tuning Tracker database alphabetically by Last Name, then apply a filter that will display the records for those customers that live in the 10010 zip code.

Hot Tip

When a table or form is saved, the last filter used is saved with it. You may reapply the filter when needed by clicking the Apply Filter button.

 # Using the Simple Query Wizard

Concept

A query is a set of instructions that you define and that Access uses to select and display data from tables and other queries. Queries are retained as an object within a database so that you can work with them whenever you like. The most common type of query is a select query, which retrieves data from one or more tables using criteria that you specify, and then displays it in a predetermined order. The Simple Query Wizard allows you to create simple select queries quickly and easily.

Do It!

Kyle will use the Simple Query Wizard to create a query which will contain all the relevant data from the database to run a mail merge to all employees.

1. Click the Queries button of the Database window to bring it to the front of the stack.

2. Click New to open the New Query dialog box, shown in **Figure 2-30**.

3. Click Simple Query Wizard to select it, then click OK. The Simple Query Wizard opens with the Employee Roster table selected in the Tables/Queries drop-down list box and a list of that table's fields in the Available Fields list box.

4. Click First Name in the Available Fields box, then click ▶ to move it to the Selected Fields box.

5. Move the following fields, in order, to the Selected Fields box in the same way that you moved the First Name field: Last Name, Street, City, State, and Zip. When you have finished, your Simple Query Wizard window should resemble the one shown in **Figure 2-31**.

6. Click Next > to go to the next step of the Simple Query Wizard. The suggested query title is selected for modification.

7. Type Mail Merge to give the query a new title, then click Finish. Access executes the query and displays it in its own window, as shown in **Figure 2-32**. It contains all the records from the Employee Roster table, but displays only the fields that you selected. Notice that the records still appear in the original order, with Klaus Busing (Employee # 001) first.

8. Click the Close button in the upper-right corner of the Select Query window to close it. The query was automatically saved by the Wizard in the final step, so it closes without prompting you to save it first.

More

There are five kinds of queries that can be created with Access. The select query, which you created in the exercise above, is the most common type. A crosstab query performs calculations and presents data in spreadsheet format, with one type of data listed down the left side and other kinds across the top. An action query is used to select records and perform operations on them, such as deleting them or placing them in new tables. A parameter query is a flexible query that prompts you to enter the selection criteria each time it is used. An SQL query is a query created using Standard Query Language statements. SQL is the basic programming language that Access uses to create and execute query procedures.

Figure 2-30 New Query dialog box

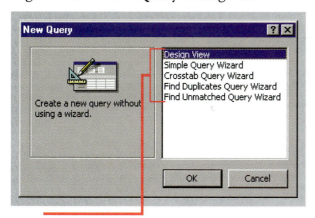

A query may be
created by any of
these methods

Moves all fields in the Selected Fields
box back to the Available Fields box,
allowing you to start over

Figure 2-31 Selected fields for simple query

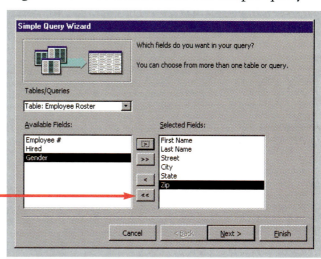

Figure 2-32 Results of Mail Merge query

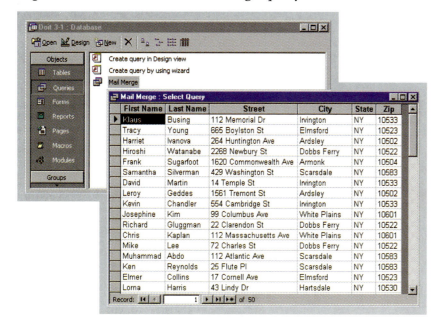

Using the Simple Query Wizard, perform a
query on the Service Records table in the
Tuning Tracker database that displays the
Customer ID # and Last Tuned fields. Name
the query **Last Tuned**.

Hot Tip

In the first step of the Simple Query
Wizard, you may add fields to the Selected
Fields box without clicking ▢ by double-
clicking the field you wish to add in the
Available fields box; double-clicking a
selected field moves it back.

Creating a Query in Design View

Concept

Design View offers more control over what gets included in a select query than the Simple Query Wizard.

Do It!

Kyle would like to create a query in Design View that lists Stay Fast's employees along with their employee numbers and the dates that they were hired.

1 Click [New] on the Queries button of the Database window to open the New Query dialog box.

2 Click [OK] to accept the default **Design View** to create a query without using a wizard. A blank Select Query window appears in the background behind the Show Table dialog box, which shows a list of the database's tables on its Tables tab.

3 Click [Add]. A small list box appears in the Select Query window listing the fields available in the table.

4 Click [Close] to close the Show Table dialog box. The Select Query window becomes active, with the insertion point blinking in the Field row.

5 Click **Employee #** in the Employee Roster list box and drag it into the Field row. When dragging, the mouse pointer will appear as a miniature field cell [▦]. When it is dropped, the field appears in the Field row, the table that it came from is displayed in the Table row, and the Show check box is checked, indicating that this field will appear in the final results of the query.

6 Double-click **Hired**, **Last Name**, and **First Name** from the Employee Roster field list in the upper-half of the Select Query window to add them as the remaining fields in the query. They will appear in the lower-half of the Select Query window, as shown in **Figure 2-33**.

7 To show the results of the query, click the Run button [!]. The query will be displayed as a table containing all records from the Employee Roster table, but displaying only the fields that you selected. The table created by the query is pictured in **Figure 2-34**.

Figure 2-33 Select Query Design View window

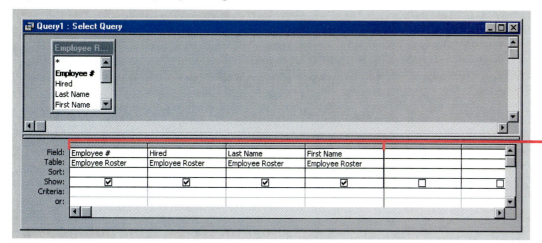

These are the fields that will appear in the query

Figure 2-34 Results of select query

Employee #	Hired	Last Name	First Name
001	6/5/93	Busing	Klaus
002	6/5/93	Young	Tracy
003	6/8/93	Ivanova	Harriet
004	6/12/93	Watanabe	Hiroshi
005	6/15/93	Sugarfoot	Frank
006	12/11/93	Silverman	Samantha
007	12/11/93	Martin	David
008	12/17/93	Geddes	Leroy
009	4/2/94	Chandler	Kevin
010	6/23/94	Kim	Josephine
011	8/13/94	Gluggman	Richard
012	8/21/94	Kaplan	Chris
013	8/21/94	Lee	Mike
014	8/23/94	Abdo	Muhammad
015	9/24/94	Reynolds	Ken
016	9/25/94	Collins	Elmer
017	12/17/94	Harris	Lorna
018	3/4/95	Nowak	Jasmine
019	4/19/95	Rosafort	Lyle
020	4/25/95	Wong	Carolyn

Record: ◄◄ ◄ 1 ► ►► ►* of 50

All fifty records have been included, though some fields are not shown

Creating a Query in Design View (continued)

Do It!

8 Click File, then click Save As. The Save As dialog box appears, as seen in **Figure 2-35**, with the default name Query1.

9 Type Employee Roster: name and date hired to name the query, then click OK to save it.

10 Click the Close button at the upper-right of the Select Query window to remove it from the screen. Notice that the query's icon appears on the Queries button of the Database window with the other query you created earlier.

More

As fields are added to the design grid in the Select Query window, a drop-down list arrow appears next to the currently selected field. You can click this list arrow to display a list of the table's available fields, as shown in **Figure 2-36**, which you can then use to select a different field. If you wish to remove a field from the design grid, click its selector button, which appears as a thin gray bar at the top of the field, and then select Delete from the Edit menu.

You can manipulate the tabular results of a query in much the same way that you would work with an actual table. You may select fields and perform a sort or a filter, or you can move columns and reorder the fields. Note that changes such as these that you make to the structure of the query do not affect the source table. However, a table generated by a select query, also called a dynaset, is dynamically linked to a source table. This means that any changes you make to the actual data in the dynaset will be reflected in the source table. Similarly, if you were to make a change to the Employee Roster table, the data in the dynaset would change to reflect it next time the query was run.

Figure 2-35 Save As dialog box

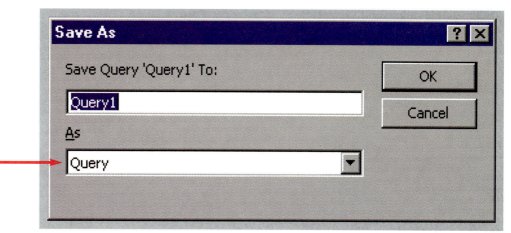

This instructs Access to save the query as an object in the same database that contains the table upon which it was based

Figure 2-36 Design grid available field drop-down list

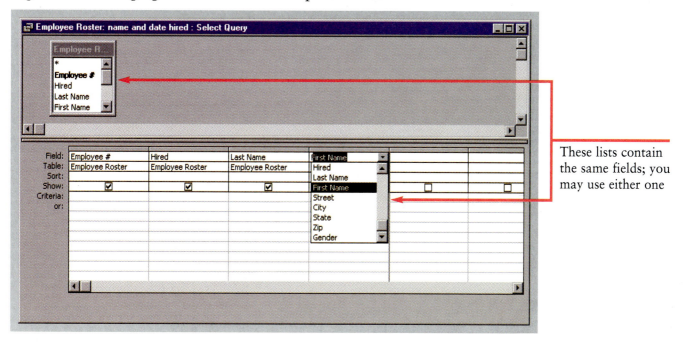

These lists contain the same fields; you may use either one

Practice

Create a query in Design View based upon the Service Records table of the Tuning Tracker database that displays the Piano Make, Piano Model, and Use fields. Name the query **Usage**.

Hot Tip

You can move and reorder fields in the Query Design window by dragging their selector buttons, just as you would in a table.

Adding Selection Criteria to a Query

Concept

After you have created a query, you may attach additional sorting and filtering criteria to it so that the table it creates shows just the data you wish to see, in the precise order in which it will be most useful.

Do It!

Kyle will now sort the query alphabetically by Last Name, move the Last Name field so that it is the leftmost field in the table, and filter the data so that only the records for those employees hired before January first of 1994 are displayed.

1 With the Employee Roster; name and date hired query selected on the Queries button of the Database window, click [Design]. The query will open in Design View.

2 Click the Sort cell in the Last Name column. An insertion point will appear in the cell along with a drop-down list arrow.

3 Click the drop-down list arrow, then select Ascending from the three choices that appear, as shown in **Figure 2-37**. This instructs Access to sort the data in the field alphabetically from A to Z.

4 Click the Run button ! on the toolbar. The query will appear in Datasheet View, sorted as specified.

5 Click the Last Name selector button to select the column, then click and drag it to the left so that it is the first column in the table.

6 Move the First Name field to make it the second column in the table, at the right of the Last Name field.

7 Click the View button to revert to Design View. Although you changed the order of the fields in the Datasheet window, this does not affect their order in the design grid. This ensures that sort criteria do not change.

8 Click the Criteria cell in the Hired field. The insertion point appears in the cell.

9 Type <1/1/94. This tell Access to display only records with dates in their Hired fields that predate January 1, 1994.

10 Click the Run button. Only those employee records that contain the specified hiring date appear, as seen in **Figure 2-38**.

11 Click the Save button to save the changes you have made, then close the Query Design View window.

More

Adding selection criteria to a query requires that you know how to use special Access symbols and words. The criteria that you set to select specific records from a table are called **conditions**, and the symbols and words you use to set these conditions are called **operators**. Access provides a number of operators for use in selection criteria. They include mathematical symbols you may already be familiar with, such as the **equal sign [=]**, the **less than sign [<]**, the **less than or equal to sign [≤]**, the **greater than sign [>]**, the **greater than or equal to sign [≥]**, and the **not equal to sign [≠]**. Access also has verbal operators such as **Between...And** which selects two values and all the values between them. You can use the **In** operator, which allows you to find fields with values that match those in a list you provide. There is also the **Like** operator, which you use to find fields that match a pattern.

When you query tables, you often use a single criterion to select records. A single selection criterion is called a **simple condition**. For example, the simple condition "equals 050" typed in the Criteria cell for the Employee # field would instruct Access to select only the record with the Employee # 050. Note that in the absence of an operator, Access assumes the equals operator, so that in this case, typing in just 50 is also acceptable.

Figure 2-37 Sort drop-down list

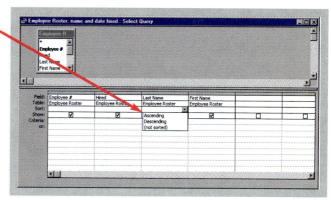

Select a sort order from the drop-down list

Figure 2-38 Query run with selection criteria

Last Name	First Name	Employee #	Hired
Busing	Klaus	001	6/5/93
Geddes	Leroy	008	12/17/93
Ivanova	Harriet	003	6/8/93
Martin	David	007	12/11/93
Silverman	Samantha	006	12/11/93
Sugarfoot	Frank	005	6/15/93
Watanabe	Hiroshi	004	6/12/93
Young	Tracy	002	6/5/93

Record: 1 of 8

Click selector button, then click and drag to move the column

Only records with Hired field values before 1/1/94 are displayed

Practice

Apply further selection criteria to the Usage query you created within the Tuning Tracker database so that only pianos with Use values greater than 3 are displayed. Save the changes you make.

Hot Tip

The **Not** operator instructs Access to select all records that do not match the criterion. For example, using the criterion Not <1/1/94 in the last exercise would have selected the records for all employees hired after the specified date instead of before.

Using Advanced Selection Criteria

Concept

Access allows you to use more than one selection criterion to a query, enabling you to select records that meet several conditions. Using more than one condition requires the use of logical operators, such as AND and OR, which allow you to connect several simple conditions together.

Do It!

To demonstrate the power of advances selection criteria, Kyle will select all records belonging to employees who were hired before 1/1/94 and whose last names also start with the letter S. He will then modify the query to select records for employees who either have last names beginning with S or were hired before 1/1/94.

1. Select the **Employee Roster; name and date hired** query on the Queries button of the Database window and click ⬚ Design ⬚. The query opens in Design View.

2. Click the Criteria cell in the Last Name field, then type **Like "S*"** into the cell. The asterisk serves as a wildcard, telling Access to select all values in the field that begin with the letter S. Since this condition was placed in the same row of the grid as the condition in the Hired field, Access will perform an AND selection, finding records that meet all the conditions.

3. Click the **Run** button ⬚ to run the query. Access displays the two records which meet all the criteria that were set, as you can see in **Figure 2-39**.

4. Click the **View** button ⬚ to return to Design View.

5. Select the **Last Name** condition, then click the **Cut** button ⬚ to send it to the Clipboard. The Windows Clipboard is a temporary storage place for data that is being moved or copied.

6. Click the **Or** cell of the **Last Name** field to place the insertion point there.

7. Click the **Paste** button ⬚ to insert the contents of the Clipboard at the insertion point, as shown in **Figure 2-40**. When you set two conditions in different rows of the design grid, Access automatically uses the OR operator to evaluate them.

8. Click the **Run** button. The query will appear with more records in its table than it had previously (**Figure 2-41**) because there are more records that match at least one of the two set conditions than meet both.

9. Click the **Close** button on the datasheet, but do **not** save changes if prompted.

More

You can further define selection queries by using combinations of AND and OR statements. For example, you could select the records for all employees who were either hired before 1/1/94 AND whose names begin with the letter S, OR who were hired after 1/1/94 AND have last names beginning with the letter R. (Refer to **Figure 2-42** to see how this would be constructed.)

Figure 2-39 Query run using a wildcard

Click to make the
next record active

Figure 2-40 Condition pasted into Or cell

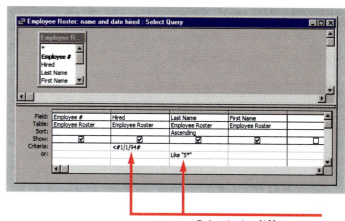

Criteria in different
rows will be applied
using the OR operator

Figure 2-41 Query run using Or operator

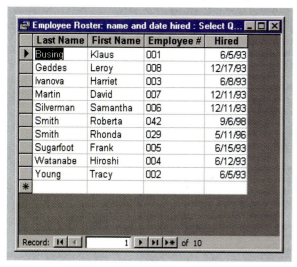

Figure 2-42 Query designed using a combination of logical operators

Field:	Employee #	Hired	Last Name	First Name
Table:	Employee Roster	Employee Roster	Employee Roster	Employee Roster
Sort:			Ascending	
Show:	☑	☑	☑	☑
Criteria:		<#1/1/94#	Like "S*"	
or:		>#1/1/94#	Like "R*"	

A combination of AND and OR statements
can be used to create more complex queries

Clearing this check box will
cause the field to be hidden
when the query is run

Practice

Further modify the Usage query in the
Tuning Tracker database to display the
records for all upright or grand pianos
made by either Steinway or Yamaha. There
should be 8 records displayed. Save the
changes you made to the query.

Hot Tip

If you had not added quotation marks
around the criterion S*, Access would have
added them anyway to indicate that it is
searching for a text item, just as it added
number signs to either end of the date in
the Hired field to indicate a numeric value.

AC 2.39

Establishing Table Relationships

Concept

One of Access' more powerful features is its ability to link tables together to create a relational database. Using a common field, you can define relationships between tables and effectively utilize them as if they were a single table. This is useful for selecting and correlating information from two or more tables.

Do It!

Kyle would like to define a relationship between the Employee Roster table and the Hours table in his database.

1 Click Tools, then click Relationships. The Show Table dialog box appears with Employee Roster table selected on the Tables tab.

2 Click [Add] to add a list box containing the selected table's fields to the Relationships window.

3 Double-click the Hours table on the Tables tab to add its list box to the Relationships window as well, then click [Close] to remove the window from the desktop.

4 Click and drag the Employee # field from the Employee Roster fields list box to the Employee # field of the Hours fields list box. The Relationships dialog box appears on the screen, as shown in **Figure 2-43**. This is how a relationship between tables is established.

5 Click the Enforce Referential Integrity check box. Referential integrity ensures that for each record in the primary table, at least one corresponding record appears in the related table. With this box checked, you cannot add records to the related table unless a matching record already exists in the primary table.

6 Click the Cascade Delete Related Records check box. With this option active, deleting a record from the primary table will automatically delete it from the related table as well.

7 Click [Create]. A line now appears between the two Employee # fields, as seen in **Figure 2-44**.

8 Click Relationships, then click Show Table. The Show Table dialog box will appear as it did before.

9 Double-click Payrates, then Position to add their field list boxes to the Relationships window, then click [Close]. The Show Table dialog box is removed from the screen.

Figure 2-43 Relationships dialog box

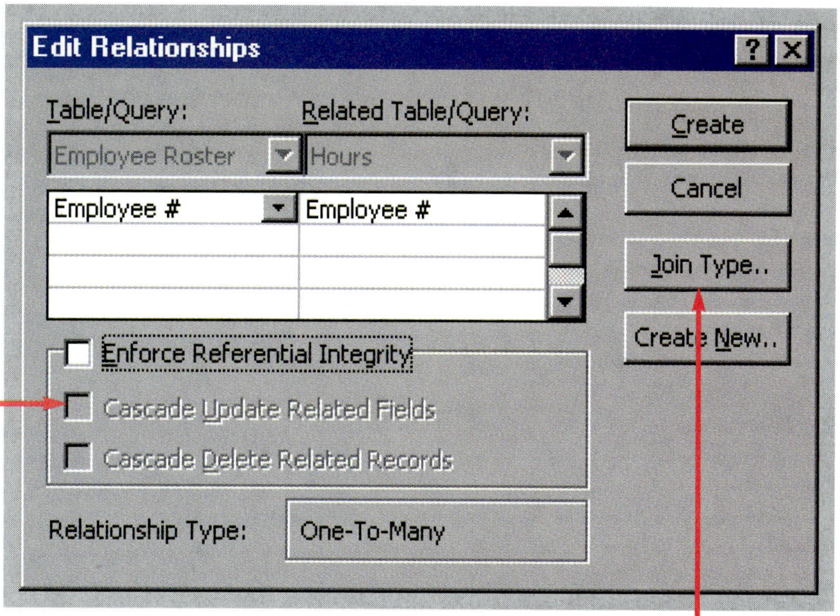

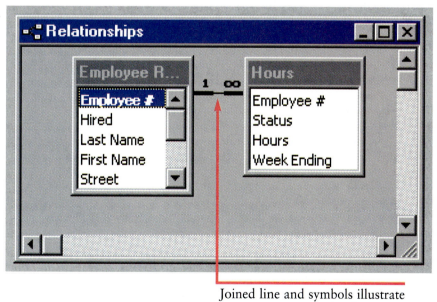

When checked, automatically updates corresponding values in a related table when they are changed in the primary table

Click to alter default join settings

Access 2000

Figure 2-44 Link between tables in Relationships window

Joined line and symbols illustrate a one-to-many relationship

AC 2.41

Establishing Table Relationships (continued)

Do It!

10 Drag the Employee # field from the Employee Roster field list box to the Employee # field of the Payrates field list box. As before, the Relationships dialog box will open.

11 Click the Enforce Referential Integrity check box and the Cascade Delete Related Records check box, then Click [Create].

12 Repeat the previous two steps to establish a similar relationship between the Employee Roster table and the Position table.

13 Click and drag the title bars of the list boxes to arrange them as they appear in **Figure 2-45**.

14 Close the Relationships window, saving changes when prompted to do so.

More

In Access, you can define three kinds of table relationships, depending on the data contained in each table. For example, the Employee Roster table and Position table have a common field, Employee #, the value of which is unique in each table. In fact, the Employee # field serves as the primary key for both tables. For each record in the Employee Roster table, there is one corresponding record in the Position table. The relationship between these two tables is known as one-to-one.

In contrast, the Employee Roster table and the Hours tables also share the Employee # field, but its value is not unique in the Hours table. In the Hours table, the Employee number is repeated and is therefore not a primary key, but a foreign key. You can still define a relationship between the tables, with each record in the Employee Roster table corresponding to two records in the Hours table. This is known as a one-to-many relationship.

The final type of relationship is called a many-to-many relationship, where many records in both tables can have many matching records in the other. Many-to-many relationships require a third table, called a junction table, that has a one-to-many relationship with the other two tables.

Figure 2-45 Relationships defined for all tables

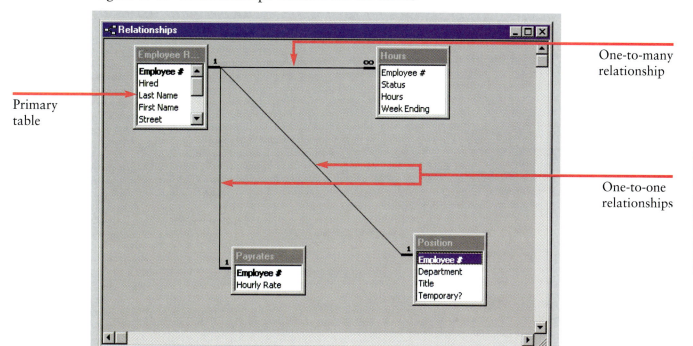

Primary table

One-to-many relationship

One-to-one relationships

Practice

Create a one-to-one relationship between the two tables in the Tuning Tracker database, Customers and Service Records. They should be linked by Customer ID #. Save the changes you make.

Hot Tip

To eliminate the relationships between your tables, click the **Clear Layout** button ⊠. To get rid of just one relationship, right-click the line between the list boxes that represents the relationship, then click Delete on the pop-up menu that appears.

Shortcuts

Function	Button/Mouse	Menu	Keyboard
Create a new database		Click File, then click New Database	[Ctrl]+[N]
Set Primary Key		Click Edit, then click Primary Key	
Switch to Datasheet View		Click View, then click Datasheet View	
Switch to Design View		Click View, then click Design View	
Save layout, design, or structural changes		Click File, then click Save	[Ctrl]+[S]
Undo		Click Edit, then click Undo	[Ctrl]+[Z]
Check spelling		Click Tools, then click Spelling	[F7]
Office Links		Click Tools, then highlight Office Links	[Ctrl]+[N]
Find		Click Edit, then click Find	[Ctrl]+[F]
Cut data to the Clipboard		Click Edit, then click Cut	[Ctrl]+[X]
Paste data from the Clipboard		Click Edit, then click Paste	[Ctrl]+[V]
Show Database window		Click Window, then click name of database	[F11]

Identify Key Features

Name the items indicated by callouts in **Figures 2-46,** and **2-47.**

Figure 2-46 Components of the Design View window

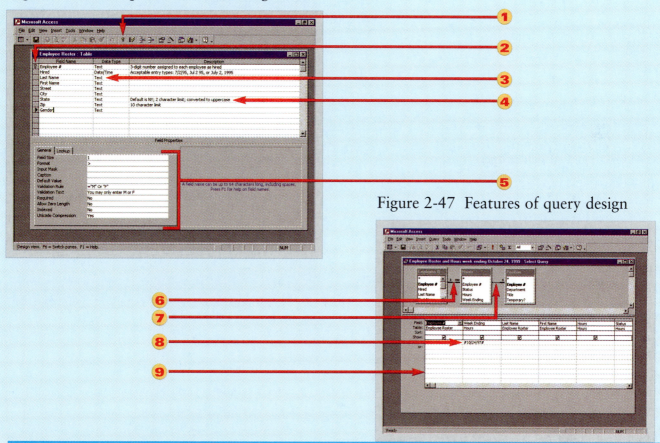

Figure 2-47 Features of query design

Select The Best Answer

10. Tells your computer what kind of information a file contains
11. Allows you to assign a field's data type and assign field properties
12. Allows you to save a database object to a new location
13. Automatically adjusts the width of a column to accommodate its widest entry
14. Restricts field entries by checking them against set conditions
15. Allows you to search for information quickly and accurately
16. Symbol used to represent unknown or unspecified data in a search or query
17. A single selection criterion
18. Expressions such as **AND** that allow you to connect several selection criteria
19. Organizes the data in a selected field from A to Z

a. Export
b. Validation Rule
c. Design View
d. File extension
e. Best Fit
f. Simple condition
g. Find command
h. Logical operators
i. Sort Ascending
j. Wildcard character

Quiz (continued)

Complete the Statement

20. All of the following are options for creating a new table except:

    a. Datasheet View

    b. Design Wizard

    c. Design View

    d. Link Table

21. To change the number of characters permitted in a field entry to a specific limit, set the:

    a. Validation Text field property

    b. Format field property

    c. Column Width field property

    d. Field Size field property

22. The character you type to instruct Access to format all entries in a field with uppercase letters is:

    a. <

    b. =

    c. >

    d. U

23. In order for a field to be used as the Primary Key, its data for each record must be:

    a. Unique and consecutive

    b. Unique and numeric

    c. Constant and numeric

    d. Constant and unique

24. Before you start working on a new database, you must first:

    a. Save it

    b. Close all other databases

    c. Import a table

    d. Export the data

25. To ensure that related tables have corresponding records, click the:

    a. Cascade Delete Related Records check box

    b. Cascade Update Related Records check box

    c. Enforce Referential Integrity check box

    d. Enforce Referential Integrity button

26. The Office Links submenu offers all of the following link options for a database except:

    a. Merge It with MS Word

    b. Analyze It with MS Excel

    c. Publish It with MS Word

    d. Merge It with MS Excel

27. To filter a table using several criteria drawn from the fields in your table, use the:

    a. Filter by Form command

    b. Filter by Selection command

    c. Filter Excluding Selection command

    d. Filter Excluding Selection button

28. A table generated by running a select query is also called a:

    a. Dynamo

    b. Related query

    c. Dynaset

    d. Parameter query

29. A table relationship can be classified as any of the following with the exception of:

    a. One-to-one

    b. One-to-many

    c. Many-to-one

    d. Many-to-many

Interactivity

Test Your Skills

1. Create a new database:

   a. Start Access from the Windows 98 taskbar.

   b. Choose the Blank Database option.

   c. Save the new database as **Test2** in the My Access Files folder.

2. Create a new database table:

   a. Choose **Design View** to construct a new table.

   b. Enter the following field names to make an address book: Last Name, First Name, Street, City, State/Province, Zip Code, Phone, Birthday.

   c. Set appropriate data types for each field.

   d. Format the Birthday field to use the **Short Date** form, and limit the Zip Code field size to 10 characters.

   e. Save the table as **Address Book**. When you are asked if you want to set a primary key, click **Yes**. Access will create an ID field which will be numbered automatically for you.

3. Work in Datasheet View:

   a. Toggle to Datasheet View.

   b. Enter records for at least 10 people (remember that the ID column will be numbered automatically).

   c. Use the **Column Width** command to **Best Fit** the first six columns in the table.

   d. Use the Best Fit shortcut (double-clicking) to adjust the remaining columns.

   e. Move the ID column to the end of the table so that it comes after the Birthday field.

   f. Save the changes you have made. Click **No** when asked if you want to test the existing data.

4. Create a new database and import database objects:

   a. Create a new database in the My Access Files folder called **Test3**.

   b. Open the Import dialog box

   c. Import the Address Book table that you created in Test2 into Test3.

   d. Design a new table that contains two fields: **ID** and **e-mail address**. Set the ID field as the **primary key** and make its data type **AutoNumber**. This table should have the same number of records as the Address Book table and they should be in the same order. If some of the people whose records you entered in the Address Book table do not have e-mail addressed, leave the field blank in the new table. Name the table **e-mail**.

Interactivity (continued)

5. Design a query:

   a. Create a new query in Design View.

   b. Choose the Address Book table from the Show Table dialog box.

   c. Design the query to display only the ID, Last Name, First Name, and Birthday fields.

   d. Run the query.

   e. Sort the resultant datasheet in ascending order by the Birthday field.

6. Establish a relationship between tables and query related tables:

   a. Open the Relationships window.

   b. Join the Address Book and e-mail tables using the ID field.

   c. Enforce Referential Integrity and activate the Cascade Delete Related Records feature.

   d. After you create the relationship, close the Relationships window, saving the changes to its layout.

   e. Design a query that displays the following information for all records: ID, Last Name, First Name, Phone, E-mail address, and Relation.

   f. Run the query and sort the data alphabetically by last name.

   g. Save the query as ADDRESS BOOK and E-MAIL: rapid communication.

Problem Solving

It is time to start building the database on magazine preferences that Ruloff and DeWitt requires. Start with a Blank Database and call it Solved2. Construct each of the three tables you planned earlier in Design View. After you finish creating each table, save it, and then switch to Datasheet View so you can enter the data you have compiled. Once you have entered the data for a table, look over the datasheet. Adjust column widths to reduce wasted space and reveal any obscured data. Decide whether the tables need to be restructured in any way, and revert to Design View if necessary. Remember that you can insert and delete fields at any time. Finally, save each table with a name that accurately describes the data that it contains.

The next part of the Magazine project will allow you to demonstrate some impressive Access skills. The Marketing and Research manager for Ruloff and DeWitt needs the following information combined: the ID number, age, gender, occupation, number of magazine titles read regularly, favorite magazine, and hobbies of each of the people you surveyed. This information must be organized by age, with a seperate datasheet for each of the following age groups: 17 and under, 18 to 34, 35 to 49, 50 to 64, and 65 and over. If an age group is not represented in your data do not create a query for it. Once you've finished this use more selection criteria to break down the database even more. When you are done, you should have one datasheet that shows all of the fields mentioned above for females 17 and under, males 17 and under, females 18-34, and so on. Save each query with a descriptive name.

Interactivity (continued)

Problem Solving

Design a database table which could be useful to you. First plan it on paper. Pick something you can use later. Perhaps you may want to keep track of your CD collection. A table of your CD collection may include fields like artist, label, number of songs, best songs, year, price, and any other information which you might find useful. If you were to do the same for your home video collection, you may want to include the length of the video, the rating, the length, and the director as some of the fields. You could create a database of all the classes you have taken at school. Some of the fields you may want to include are grades recieved, credits earned, teachers, department, cost of books. Save everything.

Once you have created your own personalized database run some queries using the data you have created. If you created a database of CD's you may want to run a query including the year of release and the cost. Choose fields which may be related and have intereset to you. For example, if you created a database of your classes and ran a query which included your grades as a field and your teachers as a field you might find that you get better grades when you have a particular teacher. You may also want to run a query to find out how many credits you have that count towards your major.

L E S S O N

3

CREATING FORMS

While tables may serve as the backbone of a database, they do not always provide the best representation of the data they contain. It is often much easier to view and work with data on your computer when its interface is that of a form. Access offers several methods of creating a form, each giving the user a different degree of guidance and control over design. AutoForm may be the quickest, easiest way to create a form, but the Form Wizard affords the greatest balance of both guidance and control.

No matter what method you use to produce a form, you can always alter it using Design View. Design View allows you to change the format of a form, and add fields graphics and records.

CASE STUDY
Kyle will now improve the functionality of his database by using the Form Wizard to design a form that Stay Fast employees will use instead of a table to enter and edit data. He will then format and edit the form in Design View.

Creating an AutoForm

Concept

Sometimes going through the Form Wizard can be confusing, and take up a lot of time. If you don't feel the need to personally select every detail of the format of your form, then you can let Access create a standardized form for you. Access will allow you to choose from three basic formats, and automatically create a standard form with fields in the order of the database you've been working in.

Do It!

Kyle will use AutoForm to create a form directly from the database he has been working in.

1 Click the Forms button to bring up options for creating a new form.

2 Click New, the New Form dialog box will open.

3 Click AutoForm: Columnar to highlight it.

4 Click Employee Roster from the drop-down arrow list, as shown in **Figure 3-1**. This tells the computer where to get the data which will be included in the form. Click OK. A standard columnar form is created with all of the fields in the order specified by the Employee Roster table (see **Figure 3-2**). Close the form and do not save your changes.

More

The form you just created was in a columnar format. AutoForm allows you to choose from three different formats, they are Columnar, Tabular, and Datasheet. The data in AutoForm will not change as long as the data is taken from the same place. The only thing that changes is the layout of the form.

Figure 3-1 New Form dialog box

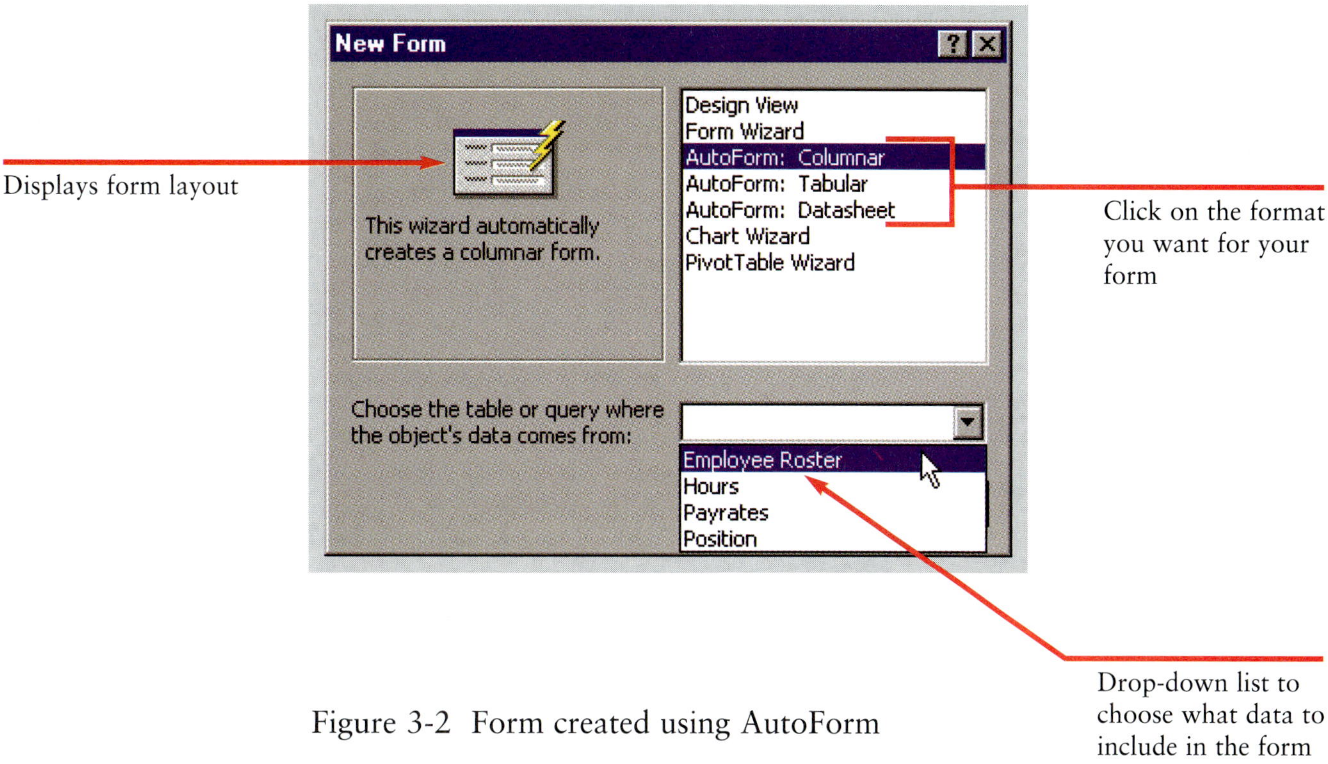

Displays form layout

Click on the format you want for your form

Drop-down list to choose what data to include in the form

Figure 3-2 Form created using AutoForm

Practice

Use AutoForm to create a tabular form that will display all fields from one of the tables in the Tuning Tracker database. Save the file under the name of the table you used.

Hot Tip

You may only use one database object to create a form using AutoForm. To create a more complex form you must use the Form Wizard, or add the fields in Design View, two skills you will learn later in this lesson.

Using the Form Wizard

Concept

AutoForm can limit the options you have when creating your form. If you want to change certain aspects of a form, or have more control over its creation use the Form Wizard to create your form.

Do It!

Kyle will use the Form Wizard to create a form that will make reading records in a table easier.

1. Click the Forms button to bring it into the Database window, then click New. The New Form dialog box will open.

2. Click Form Wizard to highlight it.

3. Click the table or query drop-down list near the bottom of the dialog box and select Employee Roster from the list that appears, then click   OK . The New Form dialog box will be replaced by the Form Wizard dialog box.

4. Click the Add All Fields button   »   to transfer all of the fields listed in the Available fields box to the Selected Fields box. Since this will be a comprehensive form, all fields in the table should be included (see **Figure 3-3**).

5. Click   Next >   to go on to the next step of the Wizard.

6. Click the Justified radio button to select it. The preview will change to reflect the chosen layout.

7. Click   Next >   to advance to the Wizard's next step.

8. Click Stone to select it. The sample form in the preview window reflects the new style.

9. Click   Next >   to advance to the Wizard's final step.

10. Click   Finish   to accept the name Access has suggested for the form, Employee Roster, and to exit the Wizard. The form is created and saved, and appears in its own window, as shown in **Figure 3-4**.

More

No Matter what format you choose to display your form in, the form still only shows one record at a time. This is the advantage of creating a form. You may scroll through each record with the record selector buttons which appear at the bottom of the form, the same as they do at the bottom of a table, so you can scroll through the form for each record.

Forms are created from the fields you select and the data you use to create them. If you use data which has been sorted the table will be sorted, only fields you select will be selected for the form.

Figure 3-3 Form Wizard dialog box

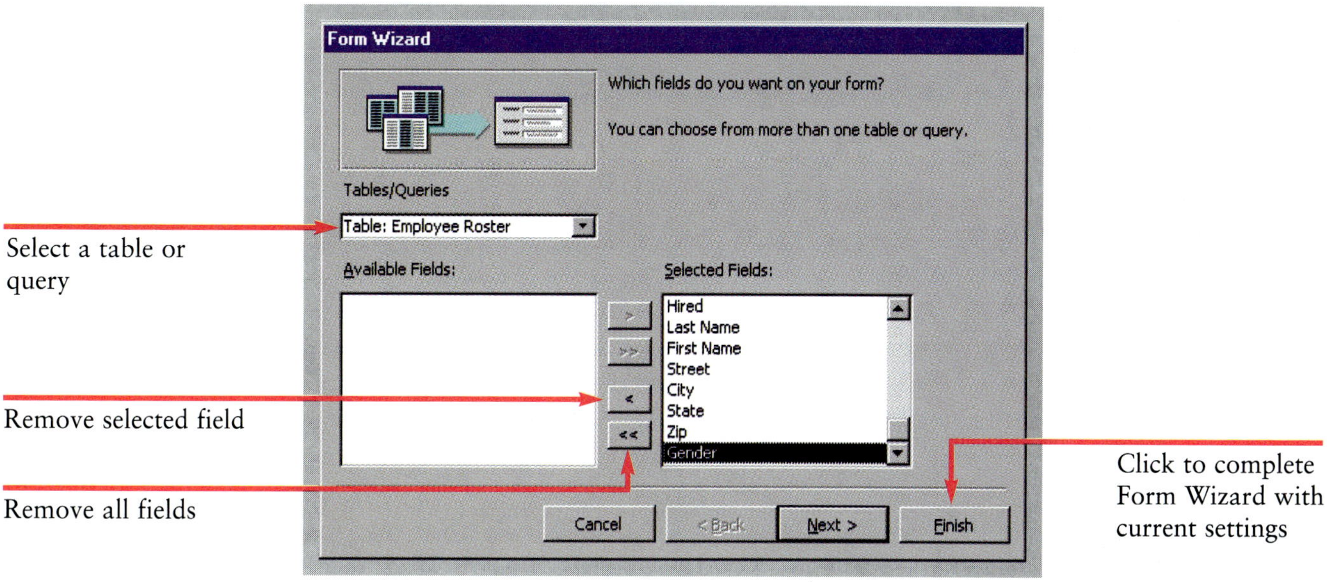

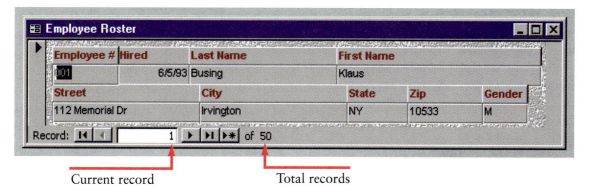

Select a table or query

Remove selected field

Remove all fields

Click to complete Form Wizard with current settings

Figure 3-4 Form created with Form Wizard

Current record

Total records

Formatting and Editing Form Elements

Concept

Once a form has been created, characteristics such as its field order, field size, and background style may be changed. These changes affect only the form itself, not the data that the form has been created to display.

Do It!

Kyle wants to customize the form he has created so that the Street field is large enough to accommodate its contents, then he will adjust the formatting so that the employee's last name will stand out. Finally, he will modify the background color of the form.

1 Click the View button ![view] to see the form in Design View. If the Toolbox toolbar appears, close it.

2 Drag the lower-right corner of the Form window downward and to the right until the entire form can be seen. As you can see in **Figure 3-5**, there are two text boxes for each field. The upper box contains the field name label, and will appear on the form as displayed. The lower box is a text box, where the field's data will be entered and displayed.

3 Click the Street field box. It now appears with sizing handles. Move the pointer over the box until it turns into a hand. Click and hold the mouse and drag the Street box, until the black line on the ruler at the top reaches 6⅛. The Street field and text box now appear to the right of the Gender field and text box.

4 While holding Shift, click the City, State, Zip, Gender, and Street field boxes. They all now appear with sizing handles. Move the pointer over the boxes until it turns into a hand. Click and hold the mouse button and drag the boxes to the leftuntil the black marker on the ruler reaches the leftmost mark on the ruler, ⅛. Your form should match the one shown in **Figure 3-6**.

5 Click in the gray area of the Design View to clear the selections you have made.

6 Click the Street box again.

7 Click the midpoint sizing handle on the right edge of the selected text box and drag it to the right until the black mark on the horizontal ruler reaches the 6 inch mark.

8 Click the Last Name text box to select it.

9 Click the Font/Fore Color drop-down list arrow ![font color], then click the blue square in the second row of the palette that appears. The placeholder text in the text box that reads "Last Name" will turn blue. Now all records on this form will display the employee's last name in blue so it will stand out from the rest of the fields.

Figure 3-5 Form in Design View

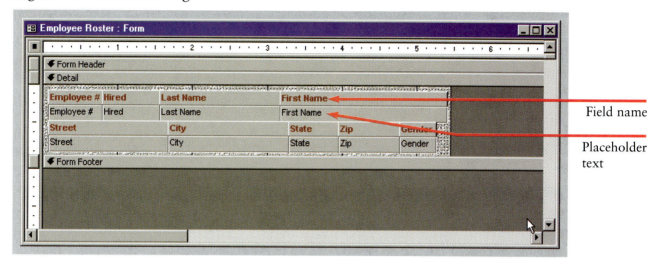

Field name

Placeholder text

Figure 3-6 A form in progress in Design View

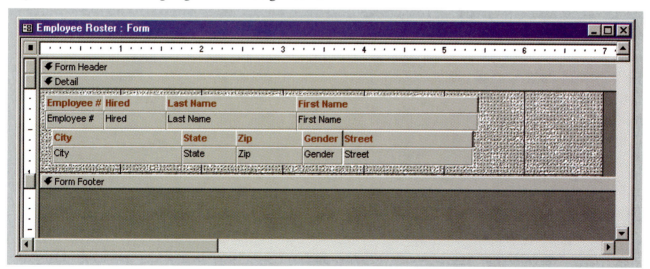

 # Formatting and Editing Form Elements (continued)

Do It!

10 Right-click the empty area of the record at the lower right, selecy Fill/Back Color from the pop-up menu that appears, and then click the pale blue square in the fourth row of the color palette. The form's background color shifts to match the selected square.

11 Click the View button to return to Form view. Your form should look like **Figure 3-7**.

More

Once selected, every item on a form may be formatted to further enhance its appearance. The Formatting toolbar, shown in **Figure 3-8**, provides control over many aspects of your form's appearance. The Object drop-down list box at the left end of the Formatting toolbar lists every item on the form; clicking a name on the list selects the corresponding item in the window. The Font and Font Size boxes, immediately to the right of the Object box, let you adjust the typeface of selected text, and the size at which it will be displayed. The Bold, Italic, and Underline buttons modify the style of selected text. The three alignment buttons, Align Left, Center, and Align Right, control the placement of text within its text box. The Formatting toolbar also contains three buttons which control the color of various form elements such as the fill or background, the text or foreground, and the lines and borders. The last two buttons on the Formatting toolbar, the Line/Border Width and Special Effects buttons, control the appearance of the lines that define a text or label box.

Figure 3-7 Formatted and edited form in Form View

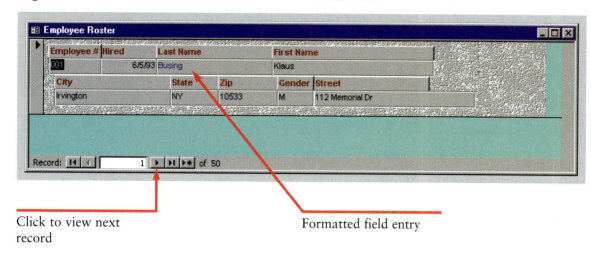

Click to view next
record

Formatted field entry

Line/Border Color

Figure 3-8 Formatting toolbar

Alignment buttons

Line/Border Width

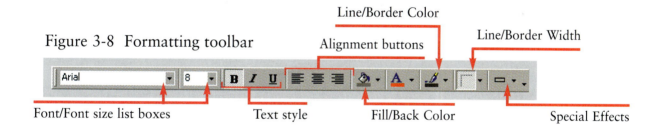

Font/Font size list boxes   Text style   Fill/Back Color   Special Effects

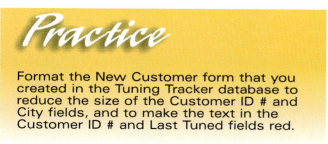

Practice

Format the New Customer form that you
created in the Tuning Tracker database to
reduce the size of the Customer ID # and
City fields, and to make the text in the
Customer ID # and Last Tuned fields red.

Hot Tip

The **AutoFormat** button ⬚ opens the
AutoFormat dialog box, which allows you
to change the template upon which a form
is based. You can choose another
predefined AutoFormat, or you can
customize your own template.

Setting Tab Order

Concept

When you enter data into a table, hitting the Tab key can help you move through your form more quickly and with greater accuracy than other methods. You may set the order in which the Tab key will bring you to the fields in your database.

Do It!

Kyle is going to set the tab order in his form so that the Street field will appear last, as it appears in the form he just created. He has also decided to place the First Name field first in the Tab order.

1. When in Design View, click View on the menu bar.

2. Click Tab Order, the Tab Order dialog box will open.

3. Click the Street row selector button as seen in **Figure 3-9**.

4. Holding down the mouse button, drag the Street field to the bottom of the Custom Order list, so it is the last field listed. Now when entering information, clicking Tab will bring you to the Street field last, as you have selected.

5. Click the First Name row selector button.

6. Holding the mose button, click and drag the First Name field to the top of the list, so it appears first.

7. Click OK.

8. Click the Form View button [icon].

9. Hit the Tab key. The order by which Tab shows you the different fields should have changed so that the Street field is last and the First Name field is first.

More

Just changing the order of a field in a form will not change the Tab order. The Tab order can be changed to whatever order you find helpful. For example, if you find that one field is changing more than any other, you can change the Tab order so that field appears first, but stays where it is with respect to its location on the form.

Figure 3-9 Tab Order dialog box

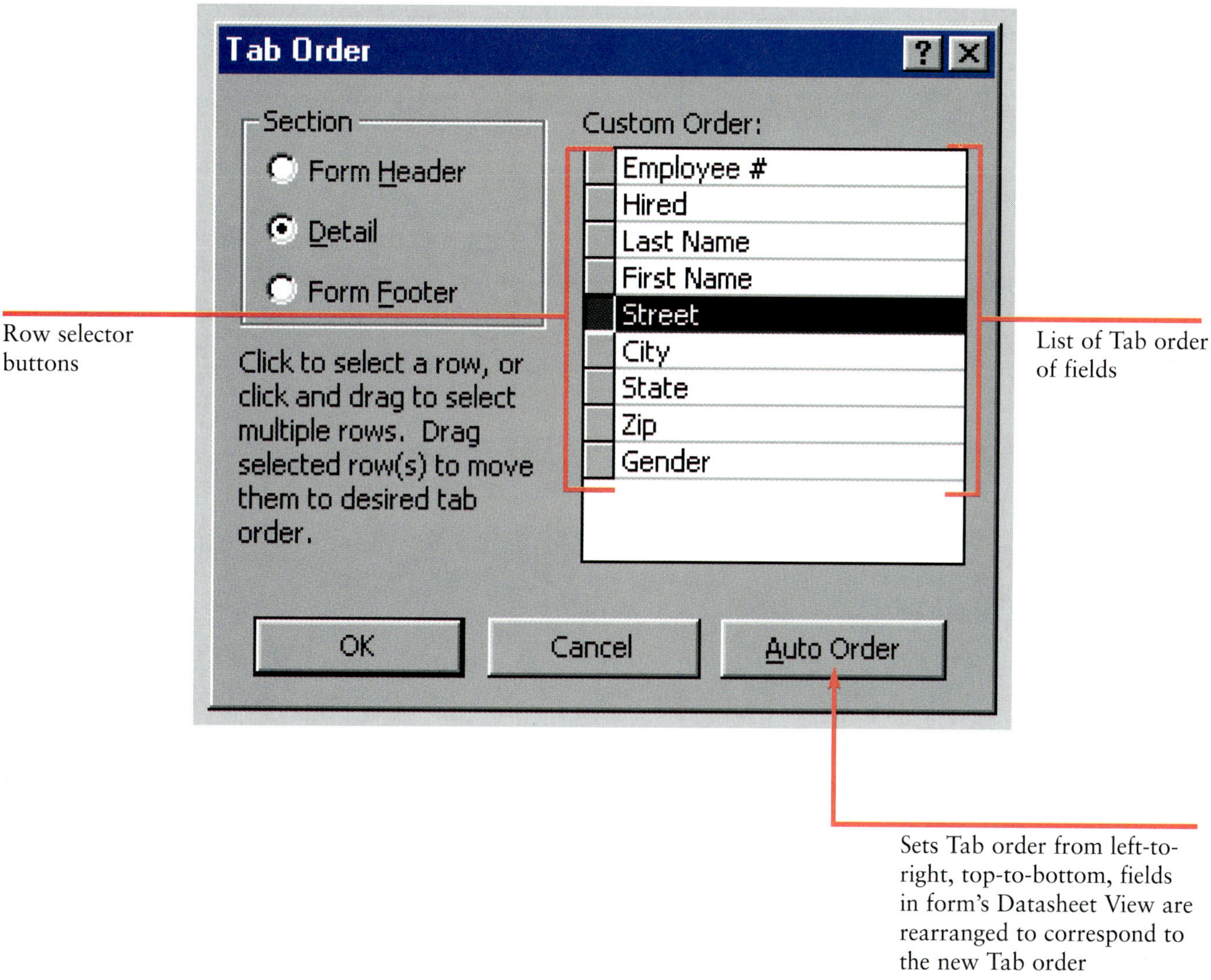

Row selector buttons

List of Tab order of fields

Sets Tab order from left-to-right, top-to-bottom, fields in form's Datasheet View are rearranged to correspond to the new Tab order

Practice

Change the Tab order of the **New Customer** form you created. Decide which fields might be used or changed most often and make those first on the list. Remember to save all of your data.

Hot Tip

Hitting **Enter** or the arrow keys has the same effect as the **Tab** key. If you customize the Tab order it will have the same effect on the other keys, as it did on the Tab key.

Modifying Controls with Expressions

Concept

Sometimes it is useful to modify the type of data which appears in a form. One way to do this is using an Expression Builder. The Expression Builder allows you to change the way data appears in a field, and what kind of data appears in a field. The data may be used to process information more efficiently.

Do It!

Kyle wants to change his form so instead of showing the date an employee was hired he can see the current date when he is working in the database.

1. Open the Employee Roster form in Design View.

2. Click the Hired text box.

3. Click the Properties button 📷 on the Design View toolbar. The Form dialog box appears. Click the Data tab to bring the Data screen to the front, as shown in Figure 3-10.

4. Click the Build button ⬛. The Expression Builder dialog box opens, the same as Figure 3-11.

5. Delete Hired from the Expressions text box.

6. Click the Commonn Expressions folder on the list in the left of the dialog box.

7. Click Current Date from the list in the middle of the dialog box.

8. Double-click Date from the list on the far right of the dialog box.

9. Click the OK button.

10. Click the Close button ⊠ on the Form dialog box, which has now turned into a Text Box dialog box.

11. Click the Form View button 🖼. Your screen should look like Figure 3-12. The Hired field box should no longer list the date hired, but instead list today's date.

More

You may also construct expressions which are mathematical in nature. Right underneath the text box in the Expressions dialog box there are buttons representing mathematical equations. You may use these buttons to construct a mathematical expression which will be formulated in the form you place it in.

If you construct an improper equation the information will not show up in the form. Make sure you have selected the correct information and the correct equation before you apply it to your form.

Figure 3-10 Form dialog box

Data tab

Build button

Change to Hired in
Form View to select
Hired

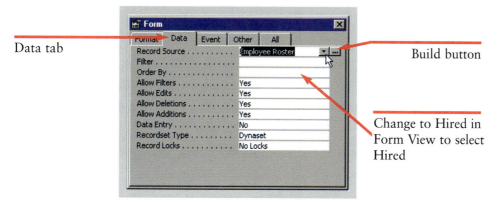

Figure 3-11 Expression Builder dialog box

List of folders to
choose from

List of fields to
choose from

List of expressions
to choose from

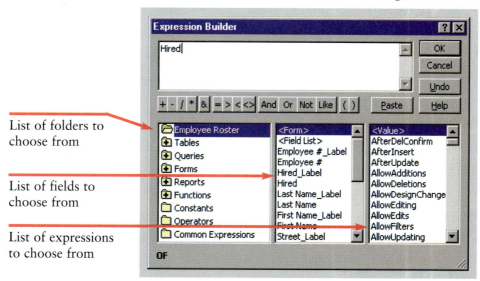

Figure 3-12 Form in Form View with expression

Expression
in a form

Practice

Add an expression to the Last Tuned field
in the **New Customer** form that you have
saved. Make the **Last Tuned** date change
to the current date when you view it in the
form. Do not save this change.

Hot Tip

Similar to the phrases you can use when
you run a query, some expressions may
contain the phrases, **And, Or, Like,** and
Not, the buttons for these phrases are
located next to the mathematical buttons in
the Expression Building dialog box.

Formatting Form Controls

Concept

You can use the same Properties options you used during the last skill to change the way data appears in a field rather than changing the actual data that appears. Instead of changing dates and numbers you can change fonts and other formatting areas.

Do It!

Kyle has decided he wants the First Name field to stand out from the rest of the fields. He is going to change the font and change other parts of its appearance to make it stand out from everything else.

1 Open the Employee Roster form in Design View.

2 Click the First Name text box, and then click the Properties button. Click the Format tab on the Form dialog box. Your screen should look like **Figure 3-13**.

3 Click the down scroll arrow until you come to the Font Name text box. Click the pointer inside the text box. Click the drop-down arrow that appears.

4 Click Courier from the drop-down list that appears.

5 Scroll down again until you reach the Font Weight text box. Click the drop-down list arrow that appears when you click the text box. Choose Heavy from the drop-down list.

6 Click the Close button on the dialog box you have been working in.

7 Click the Form view button. Your final product should look like **Figure 3-14**.

More

Formatting your form in this manner is most useful when you must change minute details, like spacing in between letters and such. When very small changes need to be made this is the better way to do them. You can still always change the font, and bold text using the Form toolbar at any time in Design View.

Make sure you are working on the correct tab, if you are on the wrong tab it is possible to make changes to your document that were not intended. If you close the program without saving changes it will revert to the last saved version.

Figure 3-13 Format tab of Form dialog box

Format tab of
Form dialog box

Drop-down list
arrow

Figure 3-14 Newly formatted form

Newly formatted
field entry

Access 2000

Practice

Change the **Font** of the **Customer ID #** field in your **New Customer** form, using the method you just learned. Save the data when you are finished.

Hot Tip

You may also choose an expression which will change the format of your form. It is possible to find expressions which will lend certain appearances or characteristics to your text.

Adding a Field

Concept

Sometimes you may find it neccessary to add a field after you have already created a form.

Do It!

Kyle has decided that he wants to put back the field which lists the date employees were hired. He is going to modify his report so his form will contain the current date, and the date hired.

1 Open the form **Employee Roster** in Design View.

2 Click the **Field List** button on the Form Design toolbar. A list of all of the fields in the form will be shown as in **Figure 3-15**.

3 Click and drag **Hired** from the list box to the form. When you drag this field the pointer will turn into a . Drag it to the right of the **First Name** label box. The field text box **Hired** will appear, as well as a label box which says **Text 18:**, that appears inside the **First Name** label box.

4 Double-click inside the **Text 18:** label box to highlight it. Delete **Text 18:** and write **Hired**. Double-click inside the original **Hired** label box, which is now being used to show the current date. Delete it and write **Date**.

5 Click the **First Name** label box to bring up the resizing handles. Click the midpoint resizing handle and drag it to the left until it reaches the edge of the **Hired** label box.

6 Click the **Hired** text box to bring up resizing handles. Click the left resizing handle and drag it to the left until it reaches the edge of the **Hired** label box. Click and drag the right sizing handle and move it to the left until the black mark on the horizontal ruler reaches 5 ½.

7 Click the Form View button . Your form should look like **Figure 3-16**.

More

All of the fields from the database the form was created from are available to add at any time. For example, if we had chosen not to include gender in our form we could have added it later, it would have been available on the same field list we saw earlier.

Figure 3-15 Field list box

List of available fields

Figure 3-16 Form with new field

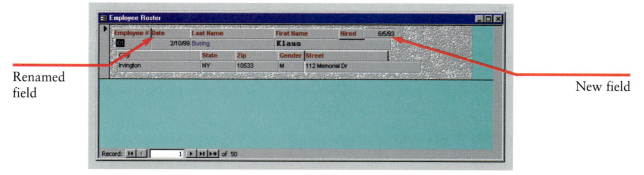

Renamed
field

New field

Access 2000

Practice

From your Student files folder open the form **Prac 3-6**. Open the form and add a field called **Odds**.

Hot Tip

The new field automatically becomes the last field in the **Tab** order, so you may find it neccessary to change the **Tab** order whenever you add a new field.

Adding Graphics to a Form

Concept

Adding graphics to your form can improve its appearance. Graphics not only make forms look more attractive, but they may also help them look more professional. Graphics can make a form look less bland.

Do It!

Kyle is going to add the logo for Stay Fast Inc. to the form he created. Kyle already has the logo saved on his computer, all he has to do is open and format it to fit the form he has created.

1. Open the form **Employee Roster** in design view.

2. Click the **Toolbox** button . The box shown if **Figure 3-17** opens.

3. Click the **Image** button . The pointer turns into . Move the pointer underneath the bottom line of the form. Underneath the **City** field. Click when you have the image where you want it. The **Insert Picture** dialog box (seen in **Figure 3-18**).

4. Choose your **Student Folder**, and click on the image marked **Stay Fast**. Click **OK**.

5. The image should be in place, you may use the pointer to click and drag the image if it is not where you want it to be.

6. Click the Form View button . Your form should look like **Figure 3-19**.

More

The safest way to save a file for inserting into a form is Bitmap, other types of image files may be inserted into forms, but some, like JPEG, TIF, and others require you to have a graphic filter installed to insert them.

If you have multiple images to insert you can do it without clicking the same toolbox button over and over. If you double-click a button on the toolbox table, it locks it down.

Use the cross part of the image pointer to line up your image. Line up the vertical and horizontal lines of the cross to line up where you want the vertical and horizontal edges of the image to begin.

Figure 3-17 Toolbox table

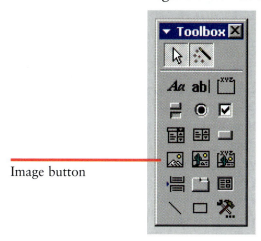

Image button

Figure 3-18 Insert Picture dialog box

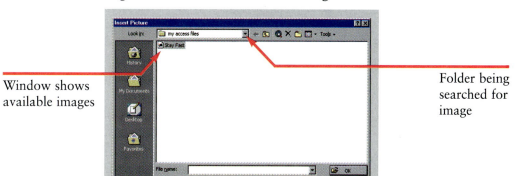

Window shows
available images

Folder being
searched for
image

Figure 3-19 Form with company logo

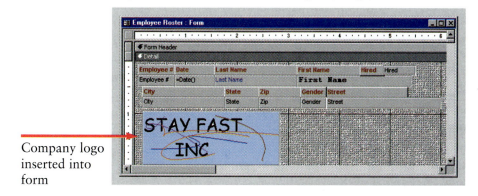

Company logo
inserted into
form

Practice

From your **Student Files** folder open the image **Prac 3-7**. Insert it into your **New Customer** form.

Hot Tip

If you click on the image at any time you may resize it with the resizing handles which appear when you click on it. You may also move the image to any location on the form once you have inserted it.

Adding a Record to a Form

Concept

Sometimes it is neccessary to update a database while you are working on a form. Access allows you to add a record to a table and database while you are working on a form.

Do It!

Stay Fast has hired someone new, and Kyle must update his form. He will do this by creating a new record in Form mode, which will also carry over to all other database modes as well.

1. Open the Employee Roster form in Form View.

2. Click the New Record button. This brings to view a blank form record. You may begin typing in the new information beginning with the new employee's first name, which is James. This is the first field in the new tab order.

3. Then type the employee # which is 051. The current date is already filled in. For Last Name type Trunk. Type the name Croton for City.

4. Type in NY, 10520, M, then 45 Wolf Rd., and 2/9/99, respectively, pressing Tab after each one. After all of the information has been added your new record should look like Figure 3-20.

More

When you must create a new record remember the way your Tab order was saved. Data will be entered in the order you set the Tab order, even if you press Enter or the arrow keys.

The new record is immediately added to the table which the form is based on. If you were to open the table that this form was based on, this new record would be added to the table.

Figure 3-20 New record in form

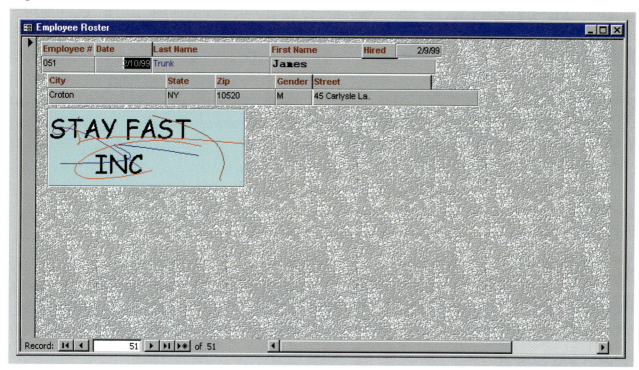

Open **Prac 3-6**. Add a new record for a horse named **Smokey**, the jockey, **Tom Dorn**, the trainer, **Joe Crash, 17 wins, $515, 089** earned, and **7:1** odds. Add this new record to that form and save it.

Hot Tip

Validation rules are still valid even if you are adding records in the form mode. Even in this mode field entries will be matched against field property specifications.

Shortcuts

Function	Button/Mouse	Menu	Keyboard
AutoForm		Click Insert, then click AutoForm (from Database window)	
Form View		Click View, then click Form View.	
Show Toolbox/ Hide Toolbox		Click View, then click Toolbox	
AutoFormat		Click Format, then click AutoFormat	
Show Field List/ Hide Field List		Click View, then click Field List	
New Record		Click Insert, then click New Record	
Properties		Click View, then click Properties	

Identify Key Features

Name the items identified by callouts in **Figure 3-21.**

Figure 3-21 Features of form in Design View

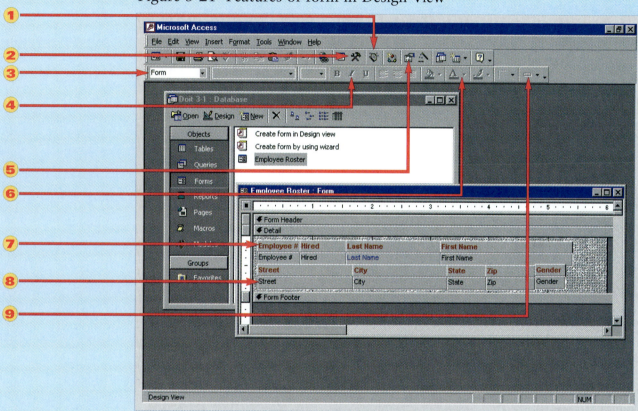

Select The Best Answer

10. Database object that displays one record at a time for easy viewing and editing

11. Contains the text options Bold, Italic, and Underline

12. Creates a standardized database object with formats selected for you

13. Changes the actual data which appears in a field

14. Puts modifications on the data that appears in a field and also its appearance.

15. Changes the way data appears in a form

16. A set of dialog boxes which create a for specifically designed for you

17. Controls the order in which data can be entered into a form

a. AutoForm

b. Format

c. Tab Order

d. Expression

e. Wizard

f. Control

g. Formatting toolbar

h. Form

Quiz (continued)

Complete the Statement

18. To create a form quickly with almost no input on its design use:
    a. The Form Wizard
    b. Design View
    c. QuickForm
    d. AutoForm

19. To view the name of every item on a form in Design View, use the:
    a. Object drop-down list
    b. View menu
    c. Field list
    d. Help menu

20. When you use the Form Wizard you can choose fields from:
    a. A single table only
    b. A single query only
    c. Tables only
    d. A combination of tables and queries

21. All of the following are layout possibilities for a form created with the Form Wizard except:
    a. Datasheet
    b. Tabular
    c. Standard
    d. Justified

22. If you want to add a record to a form after the form has already been created you may:
    a. Go back to the Database table to add the record
    b. Create a new form which includes the new record
    c. Click the New Record button
    d. Click the Record Selector button

23. To add an image to a form you must first open:
    a. The Toolbox table
    b. The View menu
    c. The Insert menu
    d. The Edit menu

24. All of the following are advantages to setting your own Tab order except:
    a. Controlling the way data is entered in a field
    b. Controlling the way data is edited in a field
    c. Quickly changing the Format of certain fields
    d. Choosing to look at the most important fields first

25. Expressions are useful for:
    a. Changing the format of certain fields
    b. Modifying the data in certain fields
    c. Changing the actual fields which appear in a form
    d. Editing new records

26. The difference between AutoForm and the Form Wizard is:
    a. AutoForm allows you more control over the appearance of a form
    b. Form Wizard allows you more control over the appearance of a form
    c. AutoForm lets you make all of the decisions which affect a form
    d. Form Wizard makes all of the decisions concerning a form for you

Interactivity

Test Your Skills

1. Create a new form using the Form Wizard:

   a. Open the database you created in the previous lesson (**Test 3**).

   b. Activate the Form Wizard.

   c. In the first step of the Wizard, add all of the fields from the Address Book table and the e-mail field from the e-mail table.

   d. When you arrive at the last step of the Wizard, choose to open the form for viewing.

2. Format and edit a form in Design View:

   a. From Form View, toggle to Design View.

   b. Apply the AutoFormat **Stone** to the form.

   c. Manipulate the fields so that **e-mail** comes directly after **Phone**.

   d. Make sure all of the field boxes are the right size, and enlarge them if neccessary so that all of the information can fit into the form.

   e. Save the form.

3. Modify the Form using Form controls:

   a. Use the form controls to manipulate the size and spacing of fields in the form.

   b. Change the look of data that appears in each field by using the form controls.

   c. Change the form controls for the e-mail field so that it only appears when you print the form.

   d. Change the format of another field by manipulating the Back Style.

4. Using the Expression Builder, change the data that appears in a field:

   a. Pick a field to change the data in, and go to the Expression Builder dialog box.

   b. Choose a way to change the data. Change it to the current date, or current time, or another expression you would like to try to build.

   c. Change the Tab order of the form, to make the field you just modified with an expression the first in the Tab order.

   d. **Do Not** save the form, and close it.

Interactivity (continued)

Problem Solving

You have done a commendable job creating a database for Ruloff and DeWitt's Marketing and Research Department. As is often the case, many people will need to access the data you have compiled. It is important, therefore, that the database has a user friendly interface, so that all members of the department are comfortable using it. Use the Form Wizard and Design View to create a form that will provide your colleagues with an effective way of working with your database's primary table.

Create AutoForms for all of the age-group queries you created for Ruloff and DeWitt. Make sure every form is saved with a descriptive name for each of the forms you create. Use the columnar format for each form. Also look at the forms in Design View to make sure that the records are sorted correctly and professionally represent the data that you want to get accross.

Create a form for your personalized database. This way it will be much easier for you to focus on each record individually instead of as part of a large table. Format it so that it is easy for you to read and access. Use the Form Wizard to create this form. You may want to exclude some fields from the form, that you don't think are neccessary, or you may also want to include every field, you must decide what is the best way to represent your database in a form.

Create an AutoForm for all of the queries you created in the last Lesson. Create tabular forms taking the data from the queries you used your databases to create. Once you have created the standard form, double check it in Design View to make sure it represents all of your data well. If you feel there are changes you need to make, make them in Design View.

LESSON

CREATING REPORTS

Frequently, it is necessary to produce paper copies of the data contained in a table or query. For this purpose, Access includes the ability to create a report, the database object most suited for printing. Like forms, reports can be created with varying amounts of input from the user. No matter what method you use to produce a form or report, you can always alter it using Design View. Access also allows you to continue to sort records and data while you are working on the database in report mode.

It is important to make sure your report will look good when it is actually printed, because what you see on your monitor is not always what you will see on the printed page. You will learn how to preview a report before you print it.

CASE STUDY
Kyle will now improve the functionality of his database by using the Report Wizard to create a company directory for Stay Fast. He will format and edit the report. When he finishes formatting the report, he will utilize the Print Preview and Page Setup features to perfect the way the report will appear on paper. Finally, Kyle will print a copy of the report.

Creating an AutoReport

Concept

If you want to create a standard report, without having to decide every attribute of it, you may create a report using AutoReport. AutoReport creates a standard report with its own specifications with the layout you want. It is the quickest way to create a report.

Do It!

Kyle is going to create an AutoReport for his Employee Roster database.

1. Click the Reports button of the Database window to open the Reports window.

2. Click New. The New Report dialog box appears.

3. Click AutoReport: Tabular.

4. From the drop-down list at the bottom of the dialog box choose Employee Roster, as in **Figure 4-1**.

5. Click OK. The dialog box closes and Access creates your standardized report, and opens it in Print Preview mode, which you will learn about later in the Lesson, which is shown in **Figure 4-2**.

More

AutoReport is an excellent, and quick way to create a clean, neat report. If you want a report which looks more stylish, or perhaps more professional you may want to put the time in to create a report using the Report Wizard.

Another limitation with the AutoReport is that you may only use one database object to create the report. When you create a report using a Wizard you may choose what fields from what databases you want to have included, but when you create an AutoReport you may choose only one database, and the report contains every field from that database.

Figure 4-1 New Report dialog box

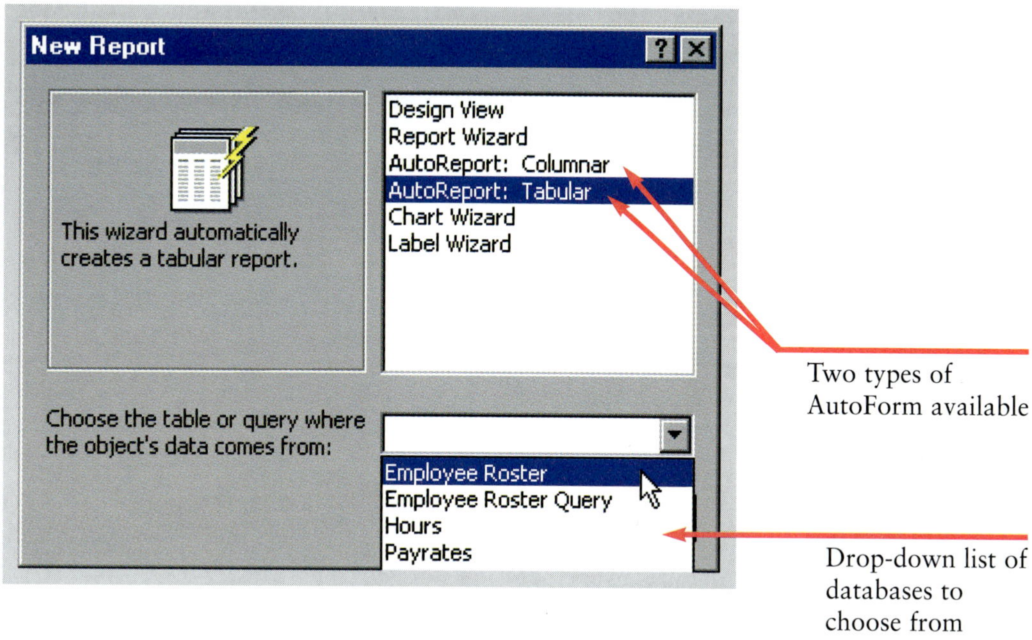

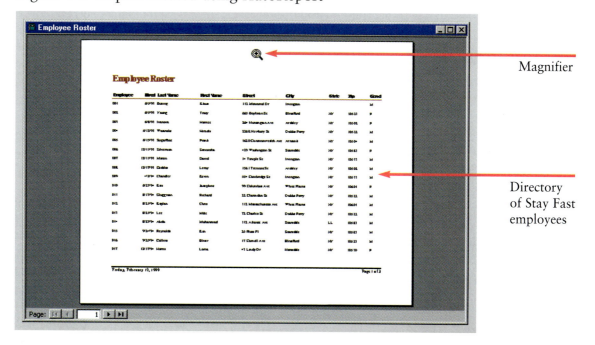

Two types of AutoForm available

Drop-down list of databases to choose from

Figure 4-2 Report created using AutoReport

Magnifier

Directory of Stay Fast employees

Access 2000

Practice

Use one of the tables from the Tuning Tracker datbase to create a columnar AutoReport. Do not save it.

Hot Tip

AutoReport is unique because when you click to create an AutoReport no dialog boxes appear, but this means your choices about your report are limited to the standard columnar or tabular report.

Using the Report Wizard

Concept

Reports are designed to effectively present your data in a printed format. Access offers control over the appearance of every item in a report to allow for design flexibility. The Report Wizard guides you through the steps necessary to create an effective report.

Do It!

Kyle will use the Report Wizard to create a company directory listing the names, addresses, and positions of all Stay Fast employees.

1. Click the **Reports** button of the Database window to bring it to the front of the stack, then click ⬚ New ⬚. The New Report dialog box appears, as shown in **Figure 4-3**.

2. Click **Report Wizard**, then click ⬚ OK ⬚. The first step of the Report Wizard appears with the Employee Roster table's fields listed in the Available Fields list box.

3. Click the **Add All Fields** button ⬚ >> ⬚ to send all the available fields to the Selected Fields list box.

4. Scroll to the top of the **Selected Fields** list box and click **Employee #** to select it.

5. Click the **Remove Field** button ⬚ < ⬚ to move the Employee # field back to the Available Fields list box, ensuring that it will not be displayed on the report.

6. Repeat the previous step to remove the **Hired** and **Gender** fields from the report. Your Selected Fields list should match the one in **Figure 4-4**.

7. To add fields from another table, click the **Tables/Queries** drop-down list box, then select **Table: Position** from the drop-down list that appears. The Available Fields list box now contains the names of the fields contained in the Position table.

8. Select the **Department** field in the Available Fields list box, then click the **Add Field** button ⬚ > ⬚ to add the Department field to the report.

9. Repeat the previous step to add the **Title** field to the report, then click ⬚ Next > ⬚. The next step of the Wizard appears asking whether you wish to apply any grouping levels.

10. Click ⬚ Next > ⬚, since you will not be adding grouping levels. The next step of the Wizard asks you to determine a sort order for fields in your report.

11. Click the first drop-down list arrow and select **Last Name** from the list that appears. The selected field will be displayed in the box, defining it as the primary sorting criterion. The second drop-down list will become active, allowing you to choose a secondary sorting criterion if you wish.

12. Click the second drop-down list arrow and select **First Name** from the field list. Records in the report will now be sorted by last name and then first name, so that if several employees share the same last name, their records will appear in the correct order. Your sorting criteria should match those in **Figure 4-5**.

Figure 4-3 New Report dialog box

Description of method selected for creating report

Click to select a table or query for report

Figure 4-4 Selected fields list

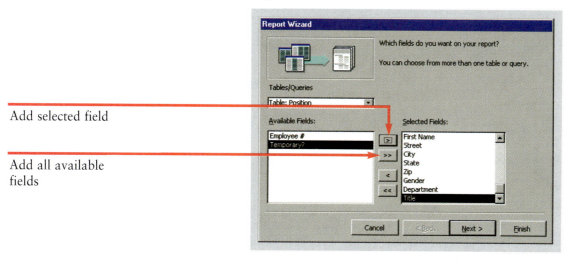

Add selected field

Add all available fields

Figure 4-5 Choosing a sort order

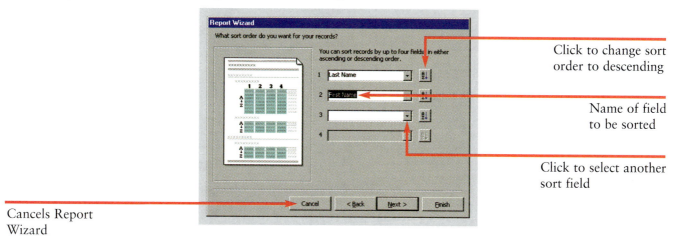

Click to change sort order to descending

Name of field to be sorted

Click to select another sort field

Cancels Report Wizard

Using the Report Wizard (continued)

Do It!

13 Click [Next >] to advance to the next step of the Wizard. This step allows you to adjust the layout of your report.

14 Click the Landscape radio button in the Orientation section. The page icon beneath the two radio buttons will change so that its width is greater than its height, indicating the way in which the report will appear on the page (see **Figure 4-6**).

15 Click [Next >]. This step of the Wizard sets the style of your report.

16 Click Bold to select the Bold style. The preview to the left of the list shows how report items will be formatted under the selected style.

17 Click [Next >] accept the Bold style and to advance to the final step of the Wizard.

18 Type Stay Fast Directory to replace the default report title, then click [Finish]. The report is saved and the Wizard closes, replaced by a window displaying the finished report in Print Preview mode, which you will learn more about later in the Lesson.

19 Click the Zoom drop-down list arrow [100% ▾] and select 75% from the list. The report is displayed at a smaller size, allowing its full width to fit within the bounds of the window, a seen in **Figure 4-7**.

More

The Report Wizard may be used to include multiple tables in a report. The same way you can when you are designing a query of a form, you may select several different tables and fields to include in your report.

The Report Wizard gives you the most options for creating a report. Its primary advantage is that you get to make all of the choices which will affect the creation of your report.

Figure 4-6 Choosing Landscape orientation

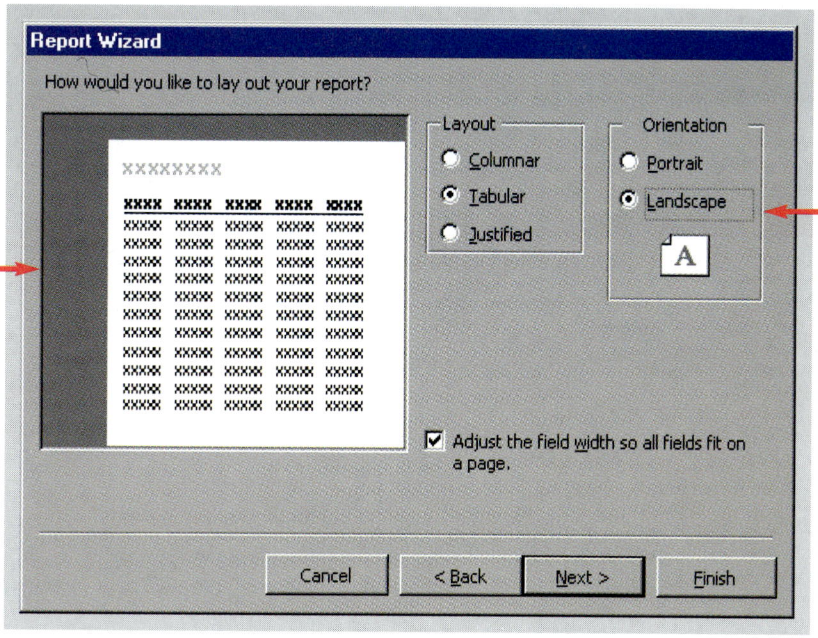

Displays preview of the selected report layout

Choose page orientation

Figure 4-7 Report displayed at 75%

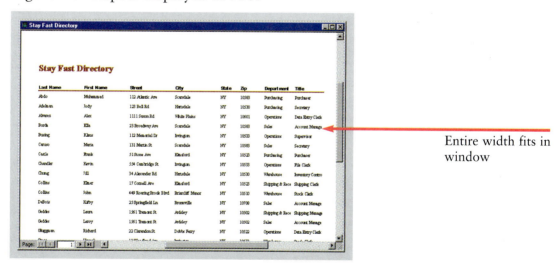

Entire width fits in window

Access 2000

Practice

Use the Report Wizard to create a columnar report based upon the Tuning Tracker database that displays the Customer ID #, First and Last Name, Piano Make and Model, and Last Tuned fields. Name it **Customer Service Report**.

Hot Tip

You may base the report on a query instead of a table. Simply choose a query in the **Tables/Queries** drop-down list in the Report Wizard dialog box.

Sorting Records in a Report

Concept

Placing records in a particular order can prove helpful when creating a report. You may sort a report using any of the fields which appear in it.

Do It!

Kyle has been asked to sort the Stay Fast Directory by job title, he will work on the report in Design View to change the sort order.

1 Open the **Stay Fast Directory** in Design View.

2 Click the **Sorting and Grouping** button ▦ from the Standard toolbar. The **Sorting and Grouping** dialog box appears.

3 Click the drop-down list arrow in the **Last Name** text box. Click **Title** from the drop-down list which appears, as shown in **Figure 4-8**. **Title** will replace **Last Name** as the first field by which the report is sorted, **First Name** will remain the second sorting field.

4 Close the **Sorting and Grouping** dialog box and return to the **Print Preview** view of the report. Click the right scroll arrow until the **Title** field is in view. Your report should look like **Figure 4-9**.

More

Changing the fields which are used to sort the records does not change the order in which the fields are displayed. Notice that although the report is sorted in ascending order of the **Title** of each employee, the field **Title** still appears as the last field, as it did before, because it was the last field chosen when you were adding fields to the report earlier.

You may also use the **Sorting and Grouping** dialog box to change the way the field is sorted from ascending to descending. Ascending will sort a field from A to Z or beginning with the lowest number, descending will sort a field from Z to A or beginning with the highest number and ending with the lowest.

Figure 4-8 Sorting and Grouping dialog box

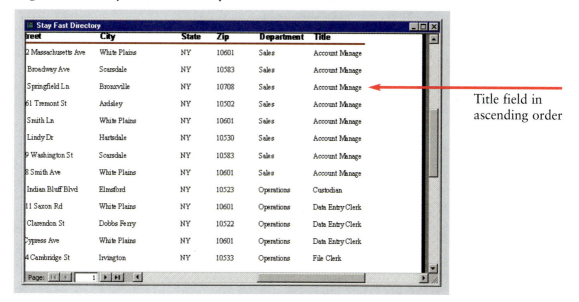

List of fields for
sorting the report

Choose the way
each field is
sorted

Figure 4-9 Stay Fast Directory in Print Preview

Title field in
ascending order

Access 2000

Practice

Change the sorting of your **Customer Service Report** so it is sorted by the **Piano Make.**

Hot Tip

You are prompted in the **Report Wizard** to choose a sort order, you can choose any field in the Wizard, and change that choice at anytime by using the **Sorting and Grouping** dialog box.

Formatting Report Elements

Concept

Like a form, all of a report's parts may be modified to alter their appearance. In Design View, you are given complete control over the formatting factors which influence the final appearance of your report.

Do It!

Kyle will alter several aspects of his report's formatting to improve its appearance.

1 Click the View button ![] on the toolbar to go to Design View, and maximize the window by clicking its Maximize button ![] if it is not already filling the application window.

2 Click Edit, then click Select All. Every element of the report will be selected, and will appear with sizing and movement handles.

3 Click the Special Effects drop-down list arrow ![], then click the Special Effect: Etched button ![] from the palette that appears. The chosen effect is applied to the borders of the text boxes, and will be more apparent in other views.

4 Click the right scroll button ![] on the horizontal scroll bar twice to reveal the right edge of the report in the window.

5 Click in the dark gray area of the window to deselect the selected items.

6 Click the following six fields while pressing [Shift]: Zip label, Zip text box, Department label, Department text box, Title label, and Title text box. They will appear selected, as shown in Figure 4-10.

7 Move the mouse pointer over the selected cells until it changes to an open hand ![], then click and drag the selected boxes (also called controls) to the right until the right corner of the black band in the horizontal ruler reaches the 9⅛ inch mark, which is the first mark to the right of the 9. The edge of the report expands to the right to accommodate the repositioned items. Moving these will allow you to expand the State label and text box controls so that the entire word will be visible.

8 Click the State label, then press [Shift] while clicking the State text box to select both controls.

9 Drag the midpoint sizing handle at the right edge of either control to the right until the black band in the horizontal ruler reaches the 6⅜ inch mark. The entire label can now be seen.

10 Click the Object drop-down list arrow on the Formatting toolbar, then click Label16 to select the report title, Stay Fast Directory, which appears in the header.

11 Click the midpoint sizing handle on the right edge of the selected control (which is all that can be currently seen in the window) to the right until it is even with the edge of the report.

12 Click the Center button ![] to center the title within its box, then click the Underline button ![] to format it with an underline, as shown in Figure 4-11.

Figure 4-10 Selected report elements

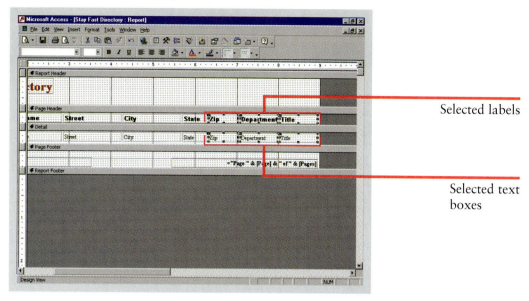

Selected labels

Selected text boxes

Figure 4-11 Formatted report label

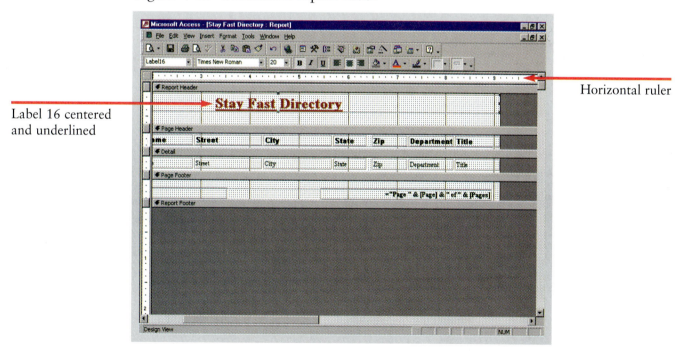

Horizontal ruler

Label 16 centered and underlined

Formatting Report Elements (continued)

Do It!

13 Use the horizontal scroll bar to scroll back to the left edge of the report.

14 Click the Object drop-down list, then click Last Name to select the Last Name text box control.

15 Click the Font/Fore Color drop-down list arrow [A], then click the blue box in the second row of the palette that appears. This will make the last names of the employees appear in blue, as they did earlier in the form you created.

16 Click the gray Page Header selector bar to select it, as pictured in Figure 4-12.

17 Click the Fill/Back Color drop-down list arrow [symbol], then click the last box in the fourth row of the palette. The background color behind the labels becomes gray.

18 Click the View button [symbol] to view the report in Print Preview mode.

19 Click the Zoom drop-down list arrow [100%] and select 75% from the list to allow the entire width of the report to fit within the boundaries of the window. Your report should resemble the one shown in Figure 4-13.

More

To increase the space between records in a report, you must increase the height of the detail section. To do so, position the mouse pointer over the bottom edge of the white space in the vertical ruler that corresponds with the details section. When the mouse pointer changes to a vertical movement pointer ↕ you can drag the bottom edge of the section downward. The extra space that is created will be repeated with each detail in the report.

There is a header and footer for both the entire report and for each page. The report header appears at the top of the first page, while the report footer appears at the bottom of the last. The page header and footer appears at the top and bottom of each page, respectively. These headers and footers are added automatically when the Report Wizard creates your report. The default page footer contains the date, the page number, and the number of total pages in the report. Items can be added to a header or footer using text box and picture box commands on the Toolbox toolbar, or may be removed by selecting their boxes and pressing [Delete].

You may choose to show or hide the header and footer of the report or of each page by selecting the appropriate command on the View menu.

Figure 4-12 Page Header selected

Appears at top of
first page of report

Appears at top of
each page

Appears at bottom
of each page

Appears at bottom
of last page of
report

Darkened to
indicate it has
been selected

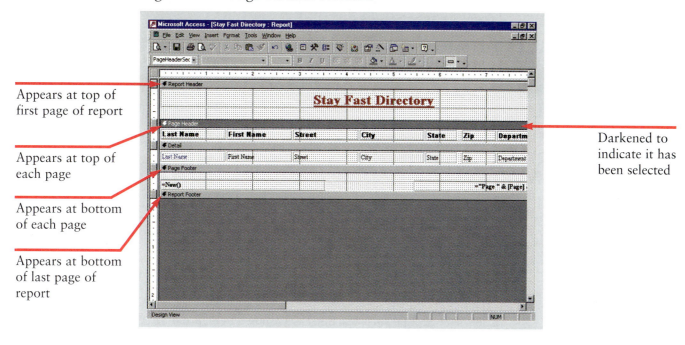

Figure 4-13 Formatted report in Print Preview at 75% zoom

Last names
formatted with
color

Page Header
with background
color filled in

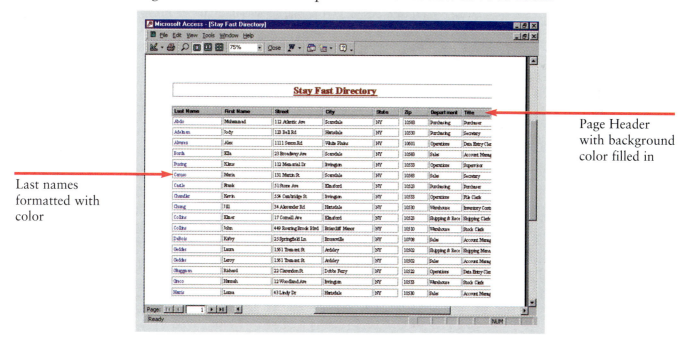

Practice

In Design View, select all the labels in the Detail section of the Customer Service Report and apply a shadowed special effect to them. Then change the background color of the Customer ID # field to yellow. Save the changes you make.

Hot Tip

In the exercise above, you used the open hand pointer to drag several selected items at once in Design View. To move just one of several selected items, grab that item's movement handle at its upper-left corner with the single item pointer ☟.

Editing Report Controls

Concept

Sometimes you may find that certain controls take up more space than others, and may need to be resized so the information is presented more efficiently. You can change the size of the controls in Design View.

Do It!

Kyle sees that the right edge of his report is being cut off because of the size of some of the titles in his title field. He is going to resize the controls so these Titles will fit onto the page.

1. Open the Stay Fast Directory in Design View.

2. While holding Shift, click the First Name label and text box. Move the pointer over the right midpoint resizing control on the text box, click and drag until the mark on the horizontal ruler reaches 2½, as shown in **Figure 4-14**.

3. Holding Shift, click the Street, City, State, Zip, Department, and Title labels and text boxes. Move the pointer over the left most text box until it turns into a hand. Click and drag the boxes until the left mark on the ruler reaches the first mark on the horizontal ruler after 2½, as shown in **Figure 4-15**.

4. Click the Title text box. Click and drag the right midpoint sizing control until the right edge meets the edge of the report.

5. Return the view to Print Preview. All of the letters in the titles should now fit onto the page, as shown in **Figure 4-16**.

6. Close the report and do not save the changes you have made.

More

If you want to change the size or placement of every elements in a report you can click Edit on the Menu toolbar, then click Select All. Once you have selected multiple elements in a report you can use any one of those elements to make changes to all of the elements. Any changes that you make to one element, the same changes will be made to every other element you selected.

You can select multiple elements without selecting all of the elements, by holding the Shift key while clicking the elements you want to select.

Figure 4-14 Resizing a label and text box in Design View

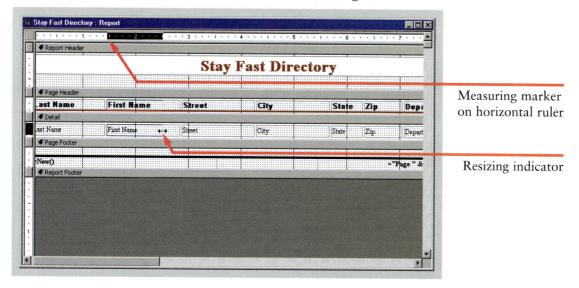

Measuring marker
on horizontal ruler

Resizing indicator

Figure 4-15 Moving elements in Design View

Resizing controls

Pointer for moving
report elements

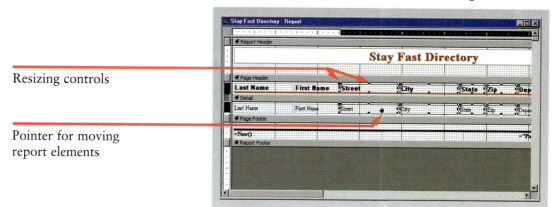

Figure 4-16 Report with edited controls

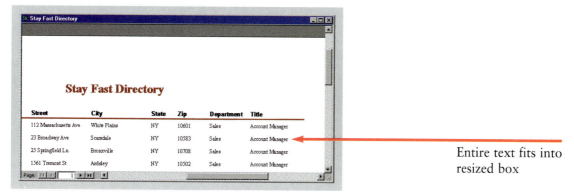

Entire text fits into
resized box

Practice

Extend the right edge of your **Customer Service Report** half inch on the horizontal ruler. Extend all of the text boxes right edges so the extra space provided is used.

Hot Tip

If you resize or relocate the label and text boxes so the right edges run over the edge of the report, Access will automatically extend the edge of the report to fit the resized boxes.

Using an Expression in a Report

Concept

Using an expression in a report may be useful to change the type of information displayed by a report. You may use mathematical expressions to change the actual data which appears or you may use an expression which doesn't alter data but adds to the report as a whole.

Do It!

Kyle would like to add an expression so the date on the report appears in the upper left corner as well as the lower-left corner of the report.

1. Open the **Stay Fast Directory** in Design View.

2. Extend the space between the Report Header and the Page Header, by moving the pointer over the Page Header box until it turns into a ✚. Then click and drag down until there is enough space to fit another text box there.

3. Use the same procedure to move the Page Footer down ⅛ on the vertical ruler. To add some space throughout the report.

4. Click the **Toolbox** button 🛠 .

5. Click the **Text box** button **abl** on the toolbox menu.

6. Use the text box pointer ⁺**abl** to create a new text box above the **First Name** label, beginning at the 1½ mark, and strecthing to the 4 mark on the horizontal ruler, as shown in **Figure 4-17**.

7. Click inside the label box on the left side of the text box you created and change the label to **Date**.

8. Click the text box, which says **Unbound** on the inside. Click the **Properties** button 🖼 .

9. Click the **Data tab** to bring it to the front of the Text dialog box which appears. Click the **Expression Builder** button **...** . This brings up the **Expression Builder** dialog box.

10. Click the **Common Expressions** folder on the left hand side list, then double click **Current Date/Time** from the middle list (shown in **Figure 4-18**).

11. Click [OK], then close the Text dialog box. Toggle back to Print Preview. The current date and time will appear in the upper-left hand corner.

More

There is a **Builder** button which appears on the Standard toolbar in Design View ◩ . It opens a dialog box which asks you what you would like to build. Choose **Expression**. You must create a text box and select it to create an expression through this method.

Figure 4-17 New text box in report

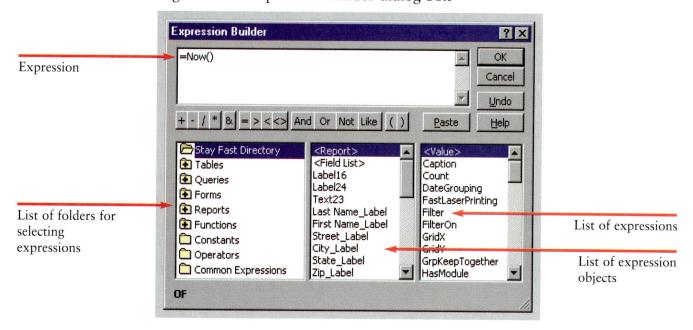

New text box and label box

Figure 4-18 Expression Builder dialog box

Expression

List of folders for selecting expressions

List of expressions

List of expression objects

Practice

Place the current date in the upper-right hand corner of your **Customer Service Report.**

Hot Tip

If expressions are not used with the proper conjunctions and tools, the data will not compute properly. When creating an expression make sure you know exactly how to compute the data, and what tools to use.

Previewing and Printing a Report

Concept

Before a document is printed, you can preview it to check for errors and to make sure it appears as you want it to. The preview shows a document exactly as it will appear on the printed page, taking into account such factors as margins, page breaks, and nonprinting items.

To create a paper or hard copy of your report, form, or other database object, it must be printed.

Do It!

Kyle wants to preview his report and fix any errors he finds. Then he will print it.

1. Click the **Multiple Pages** button 🔳 to bring up a page display palette. This palette allows you to choose the number of pages you wish to view as well as the configuration in which they will be displayed.

2. Click the page icon in the lower-right of the palette that appears to view the six pages of the report in a 2x3 configuration, shown in **Figure 4-19**. The six pages of the report will be displayed together on the screen. Three of the pages seem to be mostly blank.

3. When positioned over a page in Print Preview mode, the mouse pointer appears as the magnification pointer 🔍. Click the right edge of the first page with this pointer. The clicked area is magnified, and the plus in the magnification pointer changes to a minus, as is seen in **Figure 4-20**. As you can see, Access put the remainder of what could not fit onto a separate page.

4. Click **File**, then click **Page Setup**. The Page Setup dialog box opens on the Margins tab, as shown in **Figure 4-21**.

5. Double-click the **Left Margin** text box to select its contents.

6. Type **.75** to set the margin at three quarters of an inch, then press **[Tab]**. Your entry is formatted automatically as 0.75", the Sample changes to reflect the new margin, and the Right text box becomes selected.

Figure 4-19 Multiple pages display palette

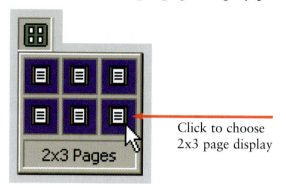

Click to choose
2x3 page display

Figure 4-20 Magnified view of pages 1 and 2

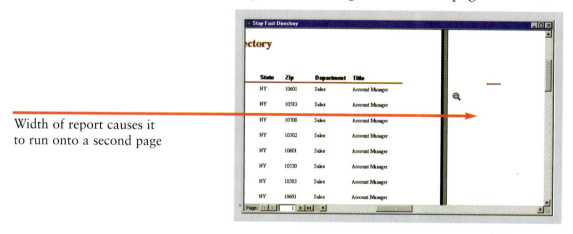

Width of report causes it
to run onto a second page

Figure 4-21 Page Setup dialog box

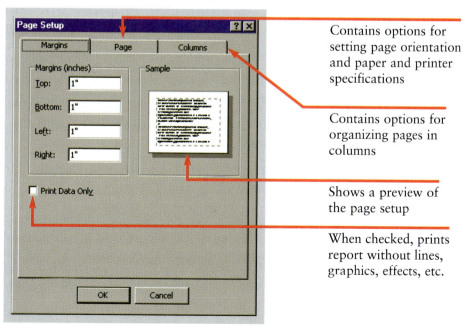

Contains options for
setting page orientation
and paper and printer
specifications

Contains options for
organizing pages in
columns

Shows a preview of
the page setup

When checked, prints
report without lines,
graphics, effects, etc.

Previewing and Printing a Report (continued)

Do It!

7 Type **.75** into the **Right** text box to adjust the margin, then click [OK]. The dialog box closes, and the new margins are applied to the document to allow each row to fit completely on each page of the report without having to spill over onto an additional page, as shown in **Figure 4-22**.

8 Click once with the demagnification pointer 🔍 to zoom out again. Notice that the report now consists of four pages instead of six, as you can see in **Figure 4-23**.

9 Click [Close] to exit Print Preview and return to Design View.

10 Click the **Save** button 🖫 to save the report with the changes you have made.

11 Click **File**, then click **Print**. The Print dialog box, shown in **Figure 4-24**, appears with the name of the last printer Access used selected.

12 After making sure that your computer is properly connected to a working printer (ask your instructor), click [OK]. Your document is sent to the printer.

13 Close the report, saving changes if prompted to do so.

14 Exit Access.

More

Changing the margins of an object with the Page Setup dialog box is only temporary; each time the object is closed, the margins will revert to their defaults. These defaults may be changed on the General tab of the Options dialog box on the Tools menu.

The Printer section of the Print dialog box tells Access which printer it is sending data to and where it is located. The Properties button opens the Printer Properties dialog box, which contains several tabs relating to paper size and orientation, print quality, and advanced options such as two-sided printing.

The Print Range section of the Print dialog box allows you to specify what portion of the document is printed. You can print the entire document or a specific range of pages; or, if you are printing a table or query, you can choose to print only the records that you had previously selected. The Copies section defines the number of copies that will be printed, and whether or not multiple copies will be collated.

Figure 4-22 Report with adjusted margins

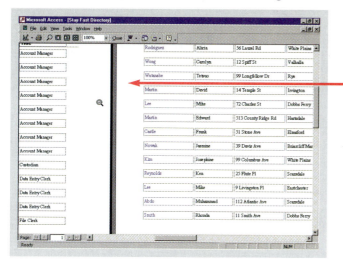

Complete records now fit on one page; page 2 now contains complete records as well

Figure 4-23 Report fit to four pages

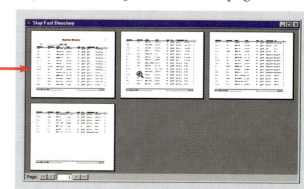

Without the spillover, report now fits on four pages

Figure 4-24 Print dialog box

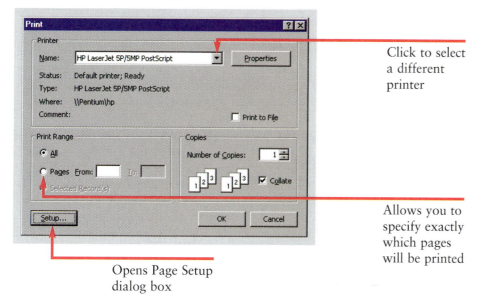

Click to select a different printer

Allows you to specify exactly which pages will be printed

Opens Page Setup dialog box

Practice

View the Customer Service Report in Print Preview, using the multiple pages button to view the report at 1x2, 2x3, and 3x4 pages. Print a copy of the Customer Service Report, then close the database and the application, saving changes if prompted.

Hot Tip

You can quickly print a database object in its entirety by selecting it in the Database window and clicking the Print button.

Access 2000

Using a Query to Generate a Report

Concept

If you have already created a query which sorts and organizes the data the way you want it, it is helpful to be able to create a report directly from a query.

Do It!

Kyle is going to use a query he created earlier to create a report, which will print the exact information he needs.

1. Click the Reports button of the Database window.

2. Click New, then click Report Wizard from the New Report dialog box. In the drop-down list choose to take the object's data from Employee Roster Query, as shown in Figure 4-25.

3. Click OK. Then click the Add All Fields button ». Click Next >.

4. Click Next >, you don't want any grouping levels.

5. At the next step of the Wizard, choose City from the first drop-down list for the first sorting field, then use Zip as the second field for sorting, as in Figure 4-26.

6. Click Next >.

7. Click the Landscape Orientation radio button, then click Next >.

8. Click Bold, then click Next >.

9. Type Directory Query to replace the default title for the report and click Finish. The report from a query is now opened in Print Preview as shown in Figure 4-27.

More

You may create a report using as many or as few fields as you want. For example, if you needed to find out how many men and women were working at Stay Fast you could create a report which simply shows whether an employee is male or female.

If this is run as a query, and you want to run the complete query as a report you should choose it as the source of data in the beginning of the Wizard, and add all fields.

Figure 4-25 New Report dialog box

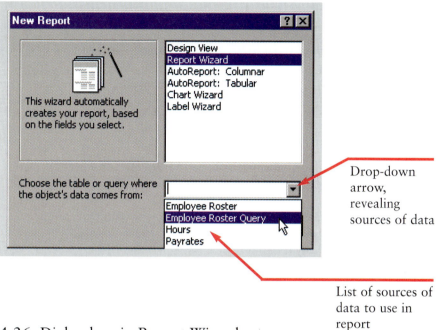

Drop-down arrow, revealing sources of data

List of sources of data to use in report

Figure 4-26 Dialog box in Report Wizard

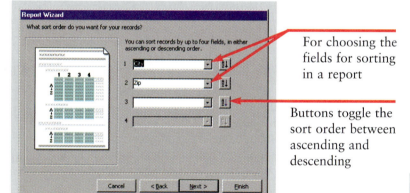

For choosing the fields for sorting in a report

Buttons toggle the sort order between ascending and descending

Figure 4-27 Report created from query

Practice

Create a report based on the query you ran in Lesson 2, **Last Tuned**. Include all of the fields from this query and save it under the title **Last Tuned Report**.

Hot Tip

You may also create an **AutoReport** from a query. When you open the new report dialog box, and choose **AutoReport**, choose to take your data from a query and your report will be automatically created.

Using the Label Wizard

Concept

Offices send out so much correspondence that one of the most productive feature of Access is its ability to create labels from databases. This is particularly useful if you have a database of customers, or suppliers who you have to send bills to. You can create labels in Access by using the Label Wizard.

Do It!

Kyle is going to create a label in the Label Wizard to customize Stay Fast's correspondence with its own employees.

1. Click New on the Reports button of the Database window.

2. Click Label Wizard, then click the drop-down arrow and choose Employee Roster as the table to get the data from.

3. Click Next > to accept the default label type. This is the first step of the Wizard, seen in Figure 4-28.

4. Click the Font Weight drop-down arrow and choose Medium from the drop-down list. Click Next >.

5. Choose Last Name and click the Add field button ›. Type "," and enter a space. Then choose First Name and click the Add field button. Type another space then choose Employee # and click the Add field button. Hit the Enter key.

6. Choose Street and hit the Add field button. Hit Enter.

7. Choose City and click the Add field button. Type "," and a space, then choose State and click the Add field button. Type a space and choose Zip and click the Add Field button. Your label prototype should look like Figure 4-29. Click Next >.

8. Choose Employee # and click the Add Field button, this sorts the labels by the Employee #. Click Next >.

9. Accept the default name for the file and click Finish. The labels you created will appear in Print Preview, sorted by the Employee # field, as in Figure 4-30.

More

In the beginning of the Label Wizard you can customize your own label. This allows you to choose the size and dimensions you want your label to have. You can choose from having dimensions in the Metric system or English system, you may choose the way the paper is fed into the printer, and the exact dimensions of the label.

Figure 4-28 Label Wizard dialog box

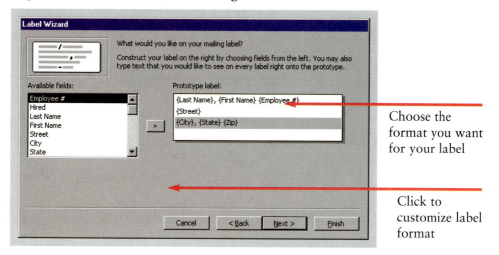

Choose the format you want for your label

Click to customize label format

Figure 4-29 Mailing label design in Label Wizard

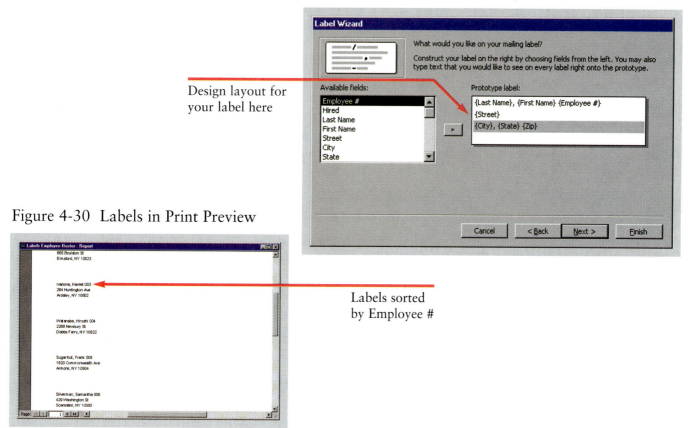

Design layout for your label here

Access 2000

Figure 4-30 Labels in Print Preview

Labels sorted by Employee #

Practice

Use one of the tables from the **Tuning Tracker** database to create a set of labels.

Hot Tip

You may also create labels from a query. When you choose where to take the data from, before you start the Wizard, choose a query and that is how the label will be created.

Shortcuts

Function	Button/Mouse	Menu	Keyboard
Show Toolbox/Hide Toolbox	🛠 🛠	Click View, then click Toolbox	
AutoFormat	🔲	Click Format, then click AutoFormat	
Show Field List/Hide Field List	🔲 🔲	Click View, then click Field List	
Zoom (Print Preview)	100% ▾	Click View, then highlight Zoom, then click value	
Fit Print Preview to Window	🔍	Click View, then highlight Zoom, then click Fit to Window	
Zoom 100%	🔍	Click View, then highlight Zoom, then click Zoom 100%	
View one, two, or multiple pages	🔲 🔲 🔲	Click View, then highlight Pages, then click number of pages	
Print Preview	🔍▾	Click View, then click Print Preview	
Print	🖨 (to bypass Print dialog box)	Click File, then click Print	Ctrl]+[P] (to open Print dialog box)

Identify Key Features

Name the items indicated by callouts in **Figure 4-31**.

Figure 4-31 Features of a report in Design View

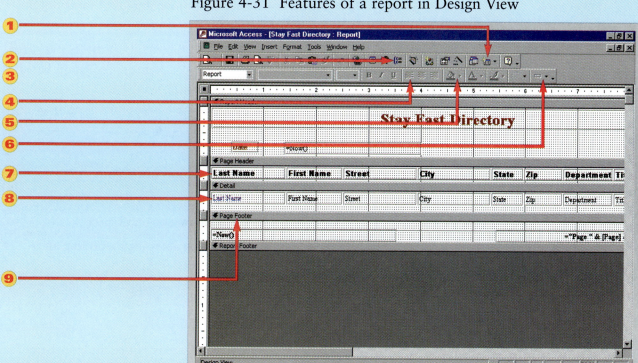

Select The Best Answer

10. Database object that formats records specifically for printing

11. Allows you to change the display size of a report for easier viewing

12. Contains the text options Bold, Italic, and Underline

13. Contains options for viewing one, two, or multiple pages

14. Controls the type of data which appears in a report

15. Changes the way in which records are presented

16. Creates labels through a series of dialog boxes which allow you to create personalized labels

17. Creates a standard report without giving you any options

a. Report

b. Wizard

c. Expression

d. AutoReport

e. Zoom

f. Sort Order

g. Formatting toolbar

h. Print Preview toolbar

Quiz (continued)

Complete the Statement

18. Reports created with the Report Wizard are automatically displayed in:

    a. Design View

    b. Print Preview

    c. Columnar style

    d. Justified style

19. To change the setup of a page so that its width is greater than its height, choose the orientation called:

    a. Portrait

    b. Landscape

    c. Horizontal

    d. Form View

20. To view the name of every item on a report in Design View, use the:

    a. Object drop-down list

    b. View menu

    c. Field List

    d. Help menu

21. When you use the Report Wizard, you can choose fields from:

    a. A single table only

    b. A single query only

    c. Tables only

    d. A combination of tables and queries

22. You may create a report using all of the following except:

    a. A query

    b. A table

    c. A label

    d. A form

23. When you create a report using AutoReport you can expect:

    a. To have a lot of input into the format of the report

    b. Access to take a long time to create the report

    c. Access to create a standardized report based on the table or query you select

    d. To control every aspect of the creation of the report

24. You may sort records in a report:

    a. Only when you use the Report Wizard

    b. Only when you use AutoReport

    c. At any time by accessing the Sorting and Grouping dialog box

    d. At any time by accessing the File menu on the menu bar

25. Using AutoReport may not be the best choice for everyone because:

    a. It limits the choices you can make about the look of a report

    b. It is difficult to find on the Standard toolbar

    c. It looks unprofessional to the people who will use and evaluate it

    d. It means you are lazy

26. You can skip the process of previewing a document before you print it by:

    a. Not creating it at all

    b. Knowing the secret code

    c. Using Access' special printing program

    d. Selecting an object in the Database window and clicking the Print button

Interactivity

Test Your Skills

1. Create a new report using the Report Wizard:

   a. Open the Report Wizard.

   b. Create a report using all of the fields from the query **ADDRESS BOOK and E-MAIL: rapid communication.**

   c. Sort the records by Last Name and then First Name, both in ascending order.

   d. When you arrive at the last step of the Wizard, choose to preview the report (if you are asked to enter a parameter value, just click OK).

2. Create a Report using AutoReport:

   a. Open the New Report dialog box.

   b. Create an AutoReport using the table **Address Book**.

   c. Take a closer look at the report in Design View.

3. Format a report in Design View:

   a. Toggle to Design View.

   b. Choose **Select All** from the Edit menu.

   c. Add the special effect **Sunken** to the report.

4. Change the way records are sorted in a report:

   a. Open the Sorting and Grouping dialog box.

   b. Sort the report using telephone numbers.

   c. Sort the telephone numbers in descending order.

5. Print a report:

   a. Return to Print Preview.

   b. Select the Print command on the File menu

   c. Click the Setup button, and then change the margins of the page from **1 inch** to **.75 inches**.

   d. Click OK to close the Page Setup dialog box.

   e. Print the report.

Access 2000

Interactivity (continued)

Problem Solving

Requests are already coming in at Ruloff and DeWitt for specific data from your database. Since these requests only require viewing the data and not changing it, paper reports would provide a convenient method of distributing the information. Use the Report Wizard and Design View to issue reports on the first three queries you created. Then, use Print Preview and the Page Setup dialog box to finalize the appearance of the reports. Lastly, print paper copies of the three objects you just created.

Open the form you created for Ruloff and DeWitt, and save it as a report. It is important that the report not take up too many pages, so make sure that you change the size of the report in Design View to make the report smaller any way you can find. Also make changes in Page Setup, change margins if you have to so that the report takes up as few pages as possible. Once you have finished formatting the report print it.

Compare and contrast the last two reports you just created and printed.

Create a report based on the personalized database table you created earlier. Create a standard tabular report using AutoReport. Once you have created the report change the sort order, sort the report by fields and in a way which you would find helpful for organizing data. Make any formatting changes that need to be made, for example if there is a field which is getting cut off, change the controls on it so it appears in its entirety. Preview and print this report.

Take the personalized form you created earlier and save it as a report. Make formatting changes so the report doesn't take up too many pages when you print it. If you need to delete images or change sizes to limit the size of each page then do so. Add an expression to this report in Design View so that every time someone looks at it, it shows them the current date and time on the upper-right side of the report. Finally, preview and print this report.

Compare and contrast the two reports you just created based on your personalized database.

Glossary

A

Action Query
A query which is used to select records and perform operations on them, such as deleting them or placing them in new tables.

Answer Wizard
One of the tabs as part of the Access help feature. Allows you to type a question, and then directs you to the help topics most closely related to your question.

AutoForm
Creates a form automatically from the table or query that you select. You can use AutoForm by selecting it from the New Form dialog box or by clicking the drop-down arrow on the New Object toolbar button.

Autoformat button
Allows you to open the Autoformat dialog box, which helps you change the template upon which a form is based, you can choose a template which is predefined or customize your own.

AutoReport
Creates a report automatically from the table or query that you select. You can use AutoReport by selecting it from the New Report dialog box or by clicking the drop-down arrow on the New Object toolbar button.

B

Best Fit
Resizes the width of a column so that it can accommodate the widest entry in the column, including the field name. You can also apply Best Fit by double-clicking the right border of a column's field name.

C

Cascade Delete Related Records
A command which, when active, ensures that deleting a record from the primary table will automatically delete it from the related table as well.

Cell
The rectangle created by the intersection of a row and a column.

Check box
A small square box that allows you to turn a dialog box option on or off by clicking it.

Clear Layout button
Allows you to eliminate relationships between tables, but does not eliminate just one relationship.

Click
To press and release a mouse button in one motion; usually refers to the left mouse button.

Close button
A button at the top-right corner of every window and box which appears in Microsoft Office, it automatically closes that particular window or box.

Column

A vertical grouping of cells that contains the values for a single field in a database table.

Contents

One of the tabs as part of the Access help features. Once clicked this tab displays the contents of the Access help feature.

Controls

The functions in databases which control the data which is presented. Editing these controls changes the way data functions are performed and the way data is represented.

Criteria

Conditions you set that instruct Access to select certain records for a query or filter.

Crosstab Query

Query which performs calculations and presents data in a spreadsheet format. It displays one type of data listed down the left side and other types of data accross the top.

D

Data

The fields, values, records, and other information entered and stored in a database.

Data type

Allows you to specify and limit what kinds of data Access will accept in a particular field.

Database

A system for storing, organizing, and retrieving information.

Database management system (DBMS)

Permits you to create a database, and then edit and manipulate its elements.

Database toolbar

Contains graphical buttons which execute specific commands when clicked.

Database window

The main control center for building and working with an Access database. Displays the database object buttons.

Datasheet

Displays the data from a table, form, or query in tabular form.

Datasheet View

Displays the table as it was created in Design View.

Default value

A field property that automatically enters an assigned value into a field for every record.

Delete Rows button

A command which allows you to delete a row from your table by clicking this button.

Design grid

The Design View grid in which you create a query or advanced filter.

Design View

The window in which you create and edit a database object.

Dialog box

A box that explains the available command options for you to review or change before executing a command.

Drag

To hold down the mouse button while moving the mouse.

Dynaset
A table which is generated from a select query, it is dynamically linked to a source table.

E

Enforce Referential Integrity
A command which ensures that for each record in the primary table, there is at least one corresponding record in the related table.

Export
Allows you to save database objects into other databases to be used there.

Expression
A mathematical equation or other form of data control which makes data entry more efficient.

Expression Builder
A dialog box offering you the option of creating a preselected expression or put an expression together yourself using the values presented.

F

Field
A column of information in a database table that contains a specific type of information.

Field list box
The small window appearing in such places as query Design View and the Relationships window that displays the fields contained in a particular table.

Field properties
Characteristics that control how a field appears, what kinds of data will be accepted in a field, and how that data will be formatted.

Field selector
The gray bar at the top of each datasheet column that contains the field name. Clicking the field selector selects the entire field.

Field size
A field property that limits the number of characters you can enter in a field.

Filter
Criteria you set that Access uses to find and display certain records.

Filter by Form
Command which allows you to select several different criteria from different tables to use to filter your table.

Filter Excluding Selection command
A filter which, when applied searches for every record which does not include the data you have specified.

Find
Allows you to locate specific types of data or specific records in database by searching for criteria which you specify.

Form
A database object that often serves as the main user interface for a database. It organizes records so that they are easy to work with.

Format
The layout of the database, including elements like fonts, sizes, styles, and dimensions. It is changeable and affects the way the entire database appears.

Form View
The view in which you work with a form, entering and editing records.

Freeze Columns command
Lets you freeze one or more columns on a datasheet so that they become the leftmost columns of your table.

G

Gallery Tab
An option available from the Office Assistant allows you to choose your Office Assistant from a list of eight.

Get External Data submenu
appears on the File menu under Import, and allows you to bring data from an external source into your Access database.

Graphics
An image which may be added to your database in the form mode. The image does not have to be a picture, but may be anything saved as an image.

H

Hide/Unhide columns
Command allows you to view the contents of a table while not viewing the borders of the columns, it literally hides, or unhides the actual columns.

I

Icon
A small graphic that identifies a button or an object.

Import
Allows you to select database objects from other databases and bring them into a new one.

Index
One of the tabs as part of the Access help feature. Allows you to type in a key word, and then directs you to a help topic which matches the keyword you typed.

Insert Rows button
A command which allows you to inset a row into a table by clicking this button.

Insertion point
A vertical blinking line that indicates where text and graphics will be inserted. The insertion point also indicates where an action will begin.

J

Junction table
A table which has a one-to-many relationship with two other tables, it is required when creating a many-to-many relationship with a third table.

L

Label
A box describing the data of the text box attatched to it.

Label Wizard
A set of dialog boxes which lead you through a series of steps ending in the creation of a prototypical label for your personal or business correspondence.

Landscape Orientation

A particular style of page orientation which creates a report on a page so that the width is greater than the height.

List box

A box from which you can choose from a number of options.

Logical operators

Operators that allow you to connect multiple simple conditions in a select query.

Mail Merge

A function which allows you to combine the fields and data from an Access database with an MS Word document.

Magnifying tool

Allows you to take a closer look at a page in Print Preview, it is controlled by the mouse and acts as the mouse pointer when in Print Preview mode.

Match Case

A command used during the Find command, forces Access to matche the capitalization of the specified search field.

Maximize

To enlarge a window to its maximum size. Maximizing an application window causes it to fill the screen; maximizing a database window causes it to fill the application window.

Menu

A list of related commands.

Menu bar

Lists the names of menus containing Access commands. Click a menu name on the menu bar to display a list of commands.

Minimize

To shrink a window to its minimum size. Minimizing an application window reduces it to a button on the taskbar; minimizing a Database window reduces it to a short title bar in the application window.

Mouse pointer

The arrow-shaped cursor on the screen that you control by guiding the mouse on your desk. You use the mouse to select and drag items, choose commands, and start or exit programs. The shape of the mouse pointer can change depending on the task being executed.

Move handle

In Design View, the large black square in the upper-left corner of a selected item. Drag the move handle to place the object in a new location.

Multiple Pages display

A mode of Print Preview which allows you to view your document as it will be seen on multiple pages. You may decide to make changes and view the effect it will have on the way the document will appear on the pages when it is printed.

Navigation buttons

The row of buttons at the bottom of a table or form used to move among records.

Object

One of the six main components of a database created in Access. Tables, queries, forms, reports, macros, modules, and pages are all database objects.

Office Assistant

An animated representation of the Microsoft Office 2000 help facility. The Office Assistant provides hints, instruction, and a convenient interface between the user and Access' various help features.

Office Links submenu

Another command which allows you to publish parts of or whole database objects in MS Word, and a Mail Merge may be created from this submenu

Operators

Symbols and words used to express conditions for selection criteria in a query.

P

Page Setup

A dialog box allowing you to change the dimensions and the layout of what your database objects will look like on the printed page.

Parameter Query

A query which is flexible and will prompt you to enter selection criteria every time the query is used.

Properties button

A button on the Formatting toolbar which allows you to add an expression to a form, and allows you to change formats of the form as well.

Primary key

A field that contains a unique and constant value for each record and can therefore be used as the common field in linked tables.

Print Preview

A view that shows how an object will appear when printed on paper. Useful for evaluating the layout of an object before printing it.

Q

Query

A database object that uses a set of instructions you provide to retrieve and display specific data from tables and other queries.

R

Radio button

A small circular button in a dialog box that allows you to switch among options.

Record

A row in a datasheet composed of all the field data for an individual entry.

Record selector

Clicking this gray box at the left edge of a datasheet record highlights the entire record.

Relational database

A database that contains multiple tables that can be linked to one another.

Relationship

The join created between two or more tables using common fields.

Remove Filter button

Undoes the filter which had previously been applied to your table, and shows all the records which appear in the table.

Report

A database object that arranges and formats data specifically for printing.

Resizing pointer

At the edges of windows the mouse pointer turns into a double headed arrow which is used by dragging to change the size of the window.

Restore button

A button on the upper-right hand side of a window or box once you have maximized or minimized it, this button restores it to its original size.

Right-click

To click the right mouse button; often used to access specialized menus and shortcuts.

Row

The horizontal grouping of data fields that forms a record in a datasheet.

Run

The command that activates a query.

S

Save As

Command in the File menu, which allows you to save documents in different files and folders, and in different modes, such as saving a form as a report.

ScreenTip

A brief description of a button or other item that appears when the mouse pointer is paused over it. Other ScreenTips are accessed by using the What's This? feature on the Help menu or by clicking the question mark button in a dialog box.

Scroll arrows

Appear at either end of the scroll bar box. Click them to scroll the scroll bar up or down to view the database you are looking at.

Scroll bar

A graphical device for moving vertically or horizontally through a database object with the mouse. Scroll bars are located along the right and bottom edges of a window.

Scroll bar box

A small grey box located inside a scroll bar that indicates your current position relative to the rest of the window. You can advance a scroll bar box by dragging it, clicking the Scroll bar on either side of it, or by clicking the Scroll arrows.

Select query

The most common type of query, used to extract and associate fields from tables and other queries and present this data in datasheet form.

Shortcut key

A keyboard equivalent of a menu command such as [Ctrl]+[S] for Save.

Shortcut menu

A pop-up menu accessed by right-clicking the mouse. The contents of the menu depend on your current activity.

Simple Condition

A single selection criterion which is used to sort records in a query.

Simple Query Wizard

A wizard which allows you to create a simple, select query quickly and easily, by helping you through a series of dialog boxes.

Sizing handles

The small black squares that appear on the border of an item when it is selected. Dragging these handles allows you to resize the object.

Sort order

The direction in which records are organized (i.e. ascending or descending).

Sorting and Grouping dialog box

Allows you to change the way a field is sorted from ascending to descending.

Specific record box
The box in the bottom left corner of a datasheet or form that indicates the number of the active record.

Standard Query Language
Programming language used by Access to create and execute queries. (SQL)

SQL Query
A query created using the Standard Query Language, the basic programming language Access uses to create and perform queries.

Status bar
The grey bar at the bottom of the window that provides information about your current activity in Access and displays the field descriptions you entered in Design View.

Tab Order
The direction in which the insertion point will move through the fields of a database object when hitting the Tab key.

Table
The object that gives a database its basic structure, storing its records and fields in tabular form.

Template
A preconstructed database. Allows you to take a database which already has its basic outline, and fill it in with your own data.

Text box
A box containing data which is text rather than objects or images.

Title bar
The horizontal bar at the top of the window that displays the name of the document or application that appears in the window.

Toolbar
A graphical bar containing buttons that act as shortcuts for common commands.

Toolbox
A toolbar that contains items you can add to a form or report in Design View.

Validation Rule
A rule which modifies the type of data which is acceptable in a database.

Validation Text
Lets the user know that the Validation Rule has been violated, and what type of data will be accepted into the database.

Value
The data that you place in a field.

W

What's This?
A help feature that allows you to click a screen item in order to receive a ScreenTip that explains the item.

Wildcard characters
Symbols that represent unknown letters or numbers when using the Find feature.

Window
A rectangular area on the screen in which you view and work on files.

Wizard
A series of specialized dialog boxes that walks you through the completion of certain tasks.

Z

Zoom
A command used in Print Preview mode while the cursor appears in the shape of a magnifying glass, allows you to take a closer look at the document in Print Preview Mode.

Index